I0213315

JUDY

TEMPLE BAILEY

1st WORLD
LIBRARY
Literary Society

Judy

Temple Bailey

© 1st World Library, 2006
PO Box 2211
Fairfield, IA 52556
www.1stworldlibrary.com
First Edition

LCCN: 2006907732

Softcover ISBN: 1-4218-2457-4
Hardcover ISBN: 1-4218-2357-8
eBook ISBN: 1-4218-2557-0

Purchase *"Judy"*
as a traditional bound book at:
www.1stWorldLibrary.com/purchase.asp?ISBN=1-4218-2457-4

1st World Library is a literary, educational organization
dedicated to:

- Creating a free internet library of downloadable ebooks

- Hosting writing competitions and offering book
publishing scholarships.

Interested in more 1st World Library books?
contact: literacy@1stworldlibrary.com
Check us out at: www.1stworldlibrary.com

1ˢᵗ World Library Literary Society

Giving Back to the World

"If you want to work on the core problem, it's early school literacy."

- James Barksdale, former CEO of Netscape

"No skill is more crucial to the future of a child, or to a democratic and prosperous society, than literacy."

- Los Angeles Times

Literacy... means far more than learning how to read and write... The aim is to transmit... knowledge and promote social participation."

- UNESCO

"Literacy is not a luxury, it is a right and a responsibility. If our world is to meet the challenges of the twenty-first century we must harness the energy and creativity of all our citizens."

- President Bill Clinton

"Parents should be encouraged to read to their children, and teachers should be equipped with all available techniques for teaching literacy, so the varying needs and capacities of individual kids can be taken into account."

- Hugh Mackay

To my father

CONTENTS

CHAPTER I

THE JUDGE AND JUDY

There was a plum-tree in the orchard, all snow and ebony against a sky of sapphire.

Becky Sharp, perched among the fragrant blossoms, crooned soft nothings to herself. Under the tree little Anne lay at full length on the tender green sod and dreamed daydreams.

"Belinda," she said to her great white cat, "Belinda, if we could fly like Becky Sharp, we would all go to Egypt and eat our lunch on the top of the pyramids."

Belinda, keeping a wary eye on a rusty red robin on a near-by stump, waved her tail conversationally.

"They used to worship cats in Egypt, Belinda," Anne went on, drowsily, "and when they died they preserved them in sweet spices and made mummies of them -"

But Belinda had lost interest. The rusty red robin was busy with a worm, and she saw her chance.

As she sneaked across the grass, Anne sat up, "I'm ashamed of you, Belinda," she said. "Becky, go bring her back!"

The tame crow fluttered from the tree with a squawk and straddled awkwardly to the stump, scaring the robin into flight, and beating an inky wing against Belinda's whiteness.

Belinda hit back viciously, but Becky flew over her head, and by several well-delivered nips sent the white cat mewing to the shelter of her mistress' arms.

"I suppose you can't help it, Belinda," said Anne, as she cuddled her, "but it's horrid of you to catch birds, horrid, Belinda."

Belinda curled down into Anne's blue gingham lap, and Becky Sharp climbed once more to the limb of the plum-tree, from which she presently sounded a discordant note.

Anne raised her head. "There is some one coming," she said, and rolled Belinda out of her lap and stood up. "Who is it, Becky?"

But Becky, having given the alarm, blinked solemnly down at her mistress, and said nothing.

"It's Judge Jameson's horse," Anne informed her pets, "and there's a girl with him, with a white hat on, and they'll stay to lunch, and there isn't a thing but bread and milk, and little grandmother is cleaning the attic."

She picked up her hat and flew through the orchard with Belinda a white streak behind her, and Becky Sharp in the rear, a pursuing black shadow.

"Little grandmother, little grandmother," called Anne, when she reached a small gray house at the edge of the orchard.

At a tiny window set in the angle of the slanting roof, a head appeared - a head tied up just now in a clean white cloth, which framed a rosy, wrinkled face.

"Little grandmother," cried Anne, breathlessly, "Judge Jameson is coming, and there isn't anything for lunch."

"There's plenty of fresh bread and milk," said the little grandmother calmly.

"But we can't give the Judge just that," said Anne.

"It isn't what you give, it's the spirit you offer it in," said the little grandmother, reprovingly. "It won't be the first time that Judge Jameson has eaten bread and milk at my table, Anne, and it won't be the last," and with that the little grandmother untied the white cloth, displaying a double row of soft gray curls that made her look like a charming, if elderly, cherub.

"You go and meet him, Anne," she said "and I'll come right down."

So Anne and Belinda and Becky Sharp went down the path to meet the carriage.

On each side of the path the spring blossoms were coming up, tulips and crocuses and hyacinths. Against the background of the gray house, an almond bush flung its branches of pink and white, and the grass was violet-starred.

"Isn't that a picture, Judy," said the Judge to the girl beside him, as they drove up, "that little old house, with the flowers and Anne and her pets?"

But Judy was looking at Anne with an uplifting of her dark, straight eyebrows.

"She must be a queer girl," she said.

"This is my granddaughter, Judy Jameson," was the Judge's introduction, when he had shaken hands with Anne. "She is going to live with me now, and I want you two to be great friends."

To little country Anne, Judy seemed like a being from another world; she had never seen anything like the white hat with its wreath of violets, the straight white linen frock, the white cloth coat, and the low ribbon-tied shoes, and the unconscious air with which all these beautiful things were worn filled her with wonder. Why, a new ribbon on her own hat always set her happy heart a-flutter!

She gave Judy a shy welcome, and Judy responded with a self-possession that made Anne's head whirl.

"My dear Judge," said the little grandmother from the doorway, "I am glad you came. Come right in."

"You are like your grandmother, my dear," she told Judy, "she and I were girls together, you know."

Judy looked at the little, bent figure in the faded purple calico. "Oh, were you," she said, indifferently, "I didn't know that grandmother ever lived in the country before she was married."

"She didn't," explained the little grandmother, "but I lived in town, and we went to our first parties together, and became engaged at the same time, and we both of us married men from this county and came up here -"

"And lived happy ever after," finished the Judge, with a smile on his fine old face, "like the people in your fairy books, Judy."

"I don't read fairy books," said Judy, with a little curve of her upper lip.

"Oh," said Anne, "don't you, don't you ever read them, Judy?"

There was such wonder, almost horror, in her tone that Judy laughed. "Oh, I don't read much," she said. "There is so much else to do, and books are a bore."

Anne looked at her with a little puzzled stare. "Don't you like books - really?" she asked, incredulously.

"I hate them," said Judy calmly.

Before Anne could recover from the shock of such a statement, the Judge waved the young people away.

"Run along, run along," he ordered, "I want to talk to Mrs. Batcheller, you show Judy around a bit, Anne."

"Anne can set the table for lunch," said the little grandmother. "Of course you'll stay, you and Judy. Take Judy with you, Anne."

Belinda and Becky Sharp followed the two girls into the dining-room. Becky perched herself on the wide window-sill in the sunshine, and Belinda sat at Judy's feet and blinked up at her.

"Belinda is awfully spoiled," said Anne, to break the stiffness, as she spread the table with a thin old cloth, "but she is such a dear we can't help it."

Judy drew her skirts away from Belinda's patting paw. "I hate cats," she said, with decision.

Anne's lips set in a firm line, but she did not say anything. Presently, however, she looked down at Belinda, who rubbed against the table leg, and as she met the affectionate glance of the cat's green orbs, her own eyes said: "I am not going to like her, Belinda," and Belinda said, "Purr-up," in polite acquiescence.

Judy had taken off her hat and coat, and she sat a slender white figure in the old rocker. Around her eyes were dark shadows of weariness, and she was very pale.

"How good the air feels," she murmured, and laid her head back against the cushion with a sigh.

Anne's heart smote her. "Aren't you feeling well, Judy?" she asked, timidly.

"I'm never well," Judy said, slowly. "I'm tired, tired to death, Anne."

Anne set the little blue bowls at the places, softly. She had never felt tired in her life, nor sick. "Wouldn't you like a glass of milk?" she asked, "and not wait until lunch is ready? It might do you good."

"I hate milk," said Judy.

Anne sat down helplessly and looked at the weary figure opposite. "I am afraid you won't have much for lunch," she quavered, at last. "We haven't anything but bread and milk."

"I don't want any lunch," said Judy, listlessly. "Don't worry about me, Anne."

But Anne went to the cupboard and brought out a precious store of peach preserves, and dished them in the little glass saucers that had been among her grandmother's wedding things. Then she cut the bread in thin slices and brought in a pitcher of milk.

"Why don't you have some flowers on the table?" said Judy. "Flowers are better than food, any day -"

Like a flame the color went over Anne's fair face. "Oh, do you like flowers, Judy?" she said, joyously. "Do you, Judy?"

Judy nodded. "I love them," she said. "Give me that big blue bowl, Anne, and I'll get you some for the table."

"Wouldn't you like a vase, Judy?" asked Anne. "We have a nice red one in the parlor."

Judy drew her shoulders together in a little shiver of distaste. "Oh, no, no," she shuddered, "this bowl is such a beauty, Anne."

"But it is so old," said Anne, "it belonged to my great-grandmother."

"That is why it is so beautiful," said Judy, as she went out of the door into the garden.

When she came in she had filled the bowl with yellow tulips, which, set in the center of the table, seemed to radiate sunshine, and to glorify the plain little room. "I should never have thought of the tulips, Judy," exclaimed Anne, "but they look lovely."

There was such genuine admiration in the tender voice, that Judy looked at Anne for the first time with interest - at the plain, straight figure in the unfashionable blue gingham, at the freckled face, with its tip-tilted nose, and at the fair hair hanging in two neat braids far below the little girl's waist.

"Do you like to live here, Anne?" she asked, suddenly.

Anne, still bending over the tulips, lifted two surprised blue eyes.

"Of course," she said. "Of course I do, Judy."

"I hate it," said Judy. "I hate the country, Anne - "

And this time she did not express her dislike indifferently, but with a swift straightening of her slender young body, and a nervous clasping of her thin white fingers.

"I hate it," she said again.

Anne stood very still by the table. What could she say to this strange girl who hated so many things, and who was staring out of the window with drawn brows and compressed red lips?

"Perhaps I like it because it is my home," she said at last, gently.

Judy caught her breath quickly. "I am never going back to my home, Anne," she said.

"Never, Judy?"

"No - grandfather says that I am to stay here with him -" There was despair in the young voice.

Anne went over to the window. "Perhaps you will like it after awhile," she said, hopefully, "the Judge is such a dear."

"I know -" Judy's tone was stifled, "but he isn't - he isn't my mother - Anne -"

For a few minutes there was silence, then Judy went on:

"You see I nursed mother all through her last illness. I was with her every minute - and - and - I want her so - I want my mother - Anne -"

But so self-controlled was she, that though her voice broke and her lips trembled, her eyes were dry. Anne reached out a plump, timid hand, and laid it over the slender one on the window-sill.

"I haven't any mother either, Judy," she said, and Judy looked down at her with a strange softness in her dark eyes. Suddenly she bent her head in a swift kiss, then drew back and squared her shoulders.

"Don't let's talk about it," she said, sharply. "I can't stand it - I can't stand it - Anne -"

But in spite of the harshness of her tone, Anne knew that there was a bond between them, and that the bond had been sealed by Judy's kiss.

CHAPTER II

ANNE GOES TO TOWN

"Grandfather," said Judy, at the lunch-table, "I want to take Anne home with us."

A little shiver went up and down Anne's spine. She wasn't sure whether it would be pleasant to go with Judy or not. Judy was so different.

"I don't believe Anne could leave Becky and Belinda," laughed the Judge. "She would have to carry her family with her."

"Of course she can leave them," was Judy's calm assertion, "and I want her, grandfather."

She said it with the air of a young princess who is in the habit of having her wishes gratified. The Judge laughed again.

"How is it, Mrs. Batcheller?" he asked.

"May Anne go?"

The little grandmother shook her head.

"I don't often let her leave me," she said.

"But I want her," said Judy, sharply, and at her tone the little grandmother's back stiffened.

"Perhaps you do, my dear," was her quiet answer, "but your wants must wait upon my decision."

The mild blue eyes met the frowning dark ones steadily, and Judy gave in. Much as she hated to own it, there was something about this little lady in faded calico that forced respect.

"Oh," she said, and sat back in her chair, limply.

The Judge looked anxiously at her disappointed face.

"Judy is so lonely," he pleaded, and Mrs. Batcheller unbent.

"Anne has her lessons."

"But to-morrow is Saturday."

"Well - she may go this time. How long do you want her to stay?"

"Until Sunday night," said the Judge. "I will bring her back in time for school on Monday."

Anne went up-stairs in a flutter of excitement. Visits were rare treats in her uneventful life, and she had never stayed at Judge Jameson's overnight, although she had often been there to tea, and the great old house had seemed the palace beautiful of her dreams.

But Judy!

"She is so different from any girl I have ever met," she explained to the little grandmother, who had followed her to her room under the eaves, and was packing her bag for her.

"Different? How?"

"Well, she isn't like Nannie May or Amelia Morrison."

"I should hope not," said the little grandmother with severity. "Nan is a tomboy, and Amelia hasn't a bit of spirit - not a bit, Anne."

Anne changed the subject, skilfully. "Do you like Judy?" she questioned.

"She is very much spoiled," said the little grandmother, slowly, "a very spoiled child, indeed. Her mother began it, and the Judge will keep it up. But Judy is like her grandmother at the same age, Anne, and her grandmother turned out to be a charming woman - it's in the blood."

"She says she is going to live with the Judge." Anne was folding her best blue ribbons, with quite a grown-up air.

"Yes. I have never told you, Anne, but the Judge's son was in the navy, and four years ago he went for a cruise and never came back."

"Was he drowned?"

"He was washed overboard during a storm, and every one except Judy believes that he was drowned. Even Judy's mother believed it in time, but Judy won't. She thinks he will come back, and so she has lived on in her old home by the sea, with a cousin of her father's for a companion - always with the hope that he will come back. But the cousin was married in the winter, and so Judy is to live with the Judge. He has always wanted it that way - but Judy clung desperately to the life in the old house by the sea. The Judge will spoil her - he can't deny her anything."

"What pretty things she has," said Anne, looking down distastefully at the simple gown and neat but plain garments that the little grandmother was packing into a shiny black bag.

The little grandmother gave her a quick look. "Never mind, dearie," she said, "just remember that you are a gentlewoman by birth, and try to be sweet and loving, and don't worry about the clothes."

But as she tied the shabby old hat with its faded roses on the fair little head, her own old eyes were wistful. "I wish I could give you pretty things, my little Anne," she whispered.

Anne gave a remorseful cry. "I don't mind, little grandmother," she said, "I don't really," and for a moment her warm young cheek lay against the soft old one.

A tiny mirror opposite reflected the two faces. "How much we look alike," cried Anne, noticing it for the first time. Then she sighed. "But my hair doesn't curl like yours, little grandmother," and in that lament was voiced the greatest trial, that had, as yet, come to Anne.

"Neither does Judy's," said Mrs. Batcheller, and Anne brightened up, but when she went down-stairs and saw Judy's bronze locks giving out wonderful lights where they were looped up with a broad black ribbon she sighed again.

When the carriage drove around, Anne caught Belinda up in her arms.

"Good-bye, pussy cat, pussy cat," she cried, "take care of grandmother, and don't catch any birds."

Belinda crooned a loving song, and tucked her pretty head under her little mistress' chin.

"You're a dear, Belinda," said Anne, "and so is Becky," and at the sound of her name the tame crow flew to Anne's shoulder and gave her a pecking kiss.

"Oh, come on," said Judy, impatiently, and the Judge lifted the shiny bag and put it on the front seat; then they waved their hands to the little grandmother and were off.

Temple Bailey

It was five miles to town, but the ride did not seem long to Anne. She pointed out all the places of interest to Judy.

"That is where I go to school," she said, as they passed a low white building at the crossroads, and later when the setting sun shone red and gold on two low glass hothouses set in the corner of a scraggly lawn, she explained their use to Judy.

"That's where Launcelot Bart raises violets," she said.

"What a funny name!" was Judy's careless rejoinder.

"Launcelot is a funny boy," said Anne, "but I think you would like him, Judy."

"I hate boys," said Judy, and settled back in the corner of the carriage with a bored air.

But Anne was eager in the defence of her friend. "Launcelot isn't like most boys," she protested, "he is sixteen, and he lived abroad until his father lost all his money, and they had to come out here, and they were awfully poor until Launcelot began to raise violets, and now he is making lots of money."

"Well, I don't want to meet him," said Judy, indifferently, "he is sure to be in the way - all boys are in the way -"

Anne did not talk much after that; but when they reached the Judge's great red brick mansion, with the white pillars and with wistaria drooping in pale mauve clusters from the upper porch, she could not restrain her enthusiasm.

"What a lovely old place it is, Judy, what a lovely, lovely place."

But Judy's clenched fist beat against the cushions. "No, it isn't, it isn't," she declared in a tense tone, so low that the Judge could not hear, "it isn't lovely. It's too big and dark and lonely, Anne - and it isn't lovely at all."

As the Judge helped them out, there came over Anne suddenly a wave of homesickness. Judy was so hard to get along with, and the Judge was so stately, and after Judy's words, even the old mansion seemed to frown on her. Back there in the quiet fields was the little gray house, back there was peace and love and contentment, and with all her heart she wished that she might fly to the shelter of the little grandmother's welcoming arms.

Perhaps something of her feeling showed in her face, for as they went up-stairs, Judy said repentantly, "Don't mind me, Anne. I'm not a bit nice sometimes - but - but - I was born that way, I guess, and I can't help it."

Anne smiled faintly. She wondered what the little grand-mother would have said to such a confession of weakness. "There isn't anything in this world that you can't help," the dear old lady would say, "and if you're born with a bad temper, why, that's all the more reason you should choose to live with a good one."

But Anne was not there to read moral lectures to her friend, and in fact as Judy opened the door of her room, the little country girl forgot everything but the scene before her.

"Oh, Judy, Judy," she cried, "how did you make it look like this? I have never seen anything like it. Never."

From where they stood they seemed to look out over the sea - a sea roughened by a fresh wind, so that tumbling whitecaps showed on the tops of the green waves. Not a ship was to be seen, not a gull swept across the hazy noon-time skies. Just water, water, everywhere, and a sense of immeasurable distance.

"It's a mirror," Judy explained, "and it reflects a picture on the other wall."

"It seems just as if I were looking out of a window," said Anne.

"I have never seen the sea, Judy. Never."

"I love it," cried Judy, "there is nothing like it in the whole world - the smell of it, and the slap of the wind against your cheeks. Oh, Anne, Anne, if we were only out there in a boat with the wind whistling through the sails." Her face was all animation now, and there was a spot of brilliant color in each cheek.

"How beautiful she is," Anne thought to herself. "How very, very beautiful."

"You must have hated to leave it," she said, presently.

"I shall never get over it," said Judy with a certain fierceness. "I want to hear the 'boom - boom - boom' of the waves - it is so quiet here, so deadly, deadly quiet -"

"How sweet your room is," said tactful little Anne, to change the subject.

"Yes, I do like this room," admitted Judy reluctantly.

There were pictures everywhere - here a dark little landscape, showing the heart of some old forest, there a flaming garden, all red and blue and purple in a glare of sunlight. In the alcove was an etching - the head of a dream-child, and a misty water-color hung over Judy's desk.

"I did that myself," she said, as Anne examined it.

"Oh, do you paint?"

"Some," modestly.

"And play?" Anne's eyes were on the little piano in the alcove.

"Yes."

"Play now," pleaded Anne.

But Judy shook her head. "After dinner," she said. "The bell is ringing now."

Dinner at Judge Jameson's was a formal affair, commencing with soup and ending with coffee. It was served in the great dining-room where silver dishes and tankards twinkled on the sideboard, and where the light came in through stained-glass windows, so that Anne always had a feeling that she was in church.

The Judge sat at the head of the table, and his sister, Mrs. Patterson, at the foot. Judy was on one side and Anne on the other, and back of them, a silent, competent butler spirited away their plates, and substituted others with a sort of sleight-of-hand dexterity that almost took Anne's breath away.

Anne and the Judge chatted together happily throughout the meal. The Judge was very fond of the earnest maiden, whose grandmother had been the friend of his youth, and his eyes went often from her sunny face to that of the moody, silent Judy. "It will do Judy good to be with Anne," he thought. "I am going to have them together as much as possible."

"Why don't you get up a picnic to-morrow?" he suggested, as Perkins passed the fingerbowls - a rite which always tried Anne's timid, inexperienced soul, as did the mysteries of the half-dozen spoons and forks that had stretched out on each side of her plate at the beginning of the meal.

"You could get some of Anne's friends to join you," went on the Judge, "and I'll let you have the three-seated wagon and Perkins; and Mary can pack a lunch."

Judy raised two calm eyes from a scrutiny of the table-cloth.

"I hate picnics," she said.

Then as the Judge, with a disappointed look on his kind old face, pushed back his chair, Judy rose and trailed languidly through the dining-room and out into the hall.

Anne started to follow, but the hurt look on the Judge's face was too much for her tender heart, and as she reached the door she turned and came back.

"I think a picnic would be lovely," she said, a little surprised at her own interference in the matter, "and - and - let's plan it, anyhow, and Judy will have a good time when she gets there."

"Do you really think she will?" said the Judge, with the light coming into his eyes.

"Yes," said Anne, "she will, and you'd better ask Nannie May and Amelia Morrison."

"And Launcelot Bart?" asked the Judge. For a moment Anne hesitated, then she answered with a sort of gentle decision.

"We can't have the picnic without Launcelot. He knows the nicest places. You ask him, Judge, and - and - I'll tell Judy."

"We will have something different, too," planned the Judge. "I will send to the city for some things - bonbons and all that. Perkins will know what to order. I haven't done anything of this kind for so long that I don't know the proper thing - but Perkins will know - he always knows -"

"Anne, Anne," came Judy's voice from the top of the stairway.

Anne fluttered away, rewarded by the Judge's beaming face, but with fear tugging at her heart. What would Judy say? Judy who hated picnics and who hated boys?

"Don't you want to come down and take a walk?" she asked coaxingly, from the foot of the stairs. It would be easier to break the news to Judy out-of-doors, and then the Judge would be in the garden, a substantial ally.

"I hate walks," said Imperiousness from the upper hall.

"Oh," murmured Faintheart from the lower hall, and sat down on the bottom step.

"I won't tell her till we are ready for bed," was her sudden conclusion.

It was getting dark, but Judy hanging over the rail could just make out the huddled blue gingham bunch.

"Aren't you coming up?" she asked, ominously.

"Yes," and with her courage all gone, Anne rose and began the long climb up the stately stairway.

CHAPTER III

IN THE JUDGE'S GARDEN

The Judge's garden was not a place of flaming flower beds and smooth clipped lawns open to the gaze of every passer-by.

It was a quiet spot. A place where old-fashioned flowers bloomed modestly in retired corners, veiled from curious stares by a high hedge of aromatic box.

There was a fountain in the Judge's garden, half-hidden by an encircling border of gold and purple fleur-de-lis, where a marble cupid rode gaily on the back of a bronze dolphin, from whose mouth spouted a stream of limpid water.

There was, too, in summer, a tangled wilderness of roses - hundred-leaved ones, and little yellow ones, and crimson ones whose tall bushes topped the hedge, and great white ones that clung lovingly to the old stone wall that was the western barrier of the garden. And there was a bed of myrtle, and another one of verbenas, over which the butterflies hovered on hot summer days, and another of pansies, and along the wall great clumps of valley lilies. And at the end of the path was a lilac bush that the Judge's wife had planted in the first days of bridal happiness.

For years it had been a lonely garden, as lonely as the old Judge's heart - for fifteen years, ever since the death of his wife, and the departure of his only son to sail the seas, the darkened windows of the old house had cast a shadow on the garden, a shadow that had fallen upon the Judge as he had walked there night after night in solitude.

But this evening as he sat on the bench under the lilac bush, a broad bar of golden light shone down upon the gay cupid and the sleeping flowers, and from the open window came the lilt of girlish laughter and the rippling strain of the "Spring Song," as Judy's fingers touched the keys of the little piano lightly.

Presently the music changed to a wild dashing strain.

"It's a Spanish dance," Judy explained to Anne. She was swaying back and forth, keeping time with her body to the melodies that tinkled from her fingers.

"I can dance it, too," she added.

"Oh, do dance it, Judy - please," cried Anne. She was living in a sort of Arabian Nights' dream. Hitherto the girls that she had known had been demure and unaccomplished, so that Judy seemed a brilliant creature, fresh from fairyland.

With a crash the music stopped, as Judy jumped up from the bench, and went into the hall.

"Move the chairs back," she directed over her shoulder, and Anne bustled about, and cleared a space in the centre of the polished floor.

In the meantime Judy bent over a great trunk in the hall.

"Oh, dear," she cried, as she piled a bewildering array of things on the floor - bright hued gowns, picturesque hats, and a miscellaneous collection of fans and ribbons. "Oh, dear, of course they are at the very bottom."

"They" proved to be a scarlet silk shawl and a pair of high-heeled scarlet slippers. Judy wound the shawl about her in the

Spanish manner, put on the high-heeled slippers, stuck an artificial red rose in her dark hair, and stepped forth as dashing a senorita as ever danced in old Seville.

"Oh, Judy," was all that Anne could say. She plumped herself down in a big chair, too happy for words, and waved to Judy to go on, while she held her breath lest she might wake from this marvelous enchantment.

Out in the garden, the Judge heard the click of castanets and the tap of the high heels.

"What is the child doing," he wondered.

As the dance proceeded, the sound of the castanets grew wilder and wilder, and the high heels beat double raps on the floor. Then, suddenly, with one sharp "click-ck" the dance ended, and there was silence.

Then Anne cried, "Do it again, do it again, Judy," and the Judge clapped his applause from the garden below.

At the sound the girls poked their heads out of the window.

"You ought to see her, Judge," Anne's tone was rapturous, "you just ought to see her."

"Shall I come down?" Judy asked. She was glowing, radiant.

"Yes, indeed. Come and dance on the path."

Five minutes later Judy was whirling, wraithlike in the white light of the moon, which turned her scarlet trappings to silver. Anne sat by the Judge and made admiring comments.

"Isn't it fine?" she asked.

The Judge nodded.

"I saw the Spanish girls do it when I was young," he said, beating time with his cane, "and Judy lived in Spain with her mother for a year, you'd think the child was born to it," and he chuckled with pride.

But when Judy came up after the last wild dash, he was more moderate in his praises. The Judge had been raised in the days when children heard often the rhyme, "Praise to the face, is open disgrace," and at times he reminded himself of the merits of such early discipline.

"I don't know what your grandmother would have thought of it, my dear," he said, with a doubtful shake of his head, "in her days, young ladies didn't do such things."

"Didn't grandmother dance?" asked Judy.

"Indeed she did," said the Judge with enthusiasm. "Why, Judy, there wasn't a couple that could beat your grandmother and me when we danced the Virginia reel."

Judy threw herself down on the bench beside him, and fanned herself with the end of her shawl.

"Can you dance," she asked, "can you really dance, grandfather? I'm so glad. Some day I shall give a party, and have all the people of the neighborhood, and we will end it with the reel. May I, grandfather?"

"You may do anything you wish," was the Judge's rash promise, and with a quick laugh, Judy saw her opportunity and took advantage of it.

"Then let's go down to the kitchen," she said, "and get something to eat now. I didn't eat much dinner, and I am starved. Aren't you, Anne?"

But Anne had been trained in the way she should go. "I - I haven't thought of being hungry," she hesitated. "I never eat before I go to bed."

"Oh, I do," said Judy, scornfully. "And dancing makes me ravenous."

"But Perkins has retired, and Mary, and everybody -" expostulated the Judge.

"Who cares for Perkins?" asked Judy with her nose in the air.

"Well," said the Judge, who was hopelessly the slave of his servants, "he might not like it -"

"Judge Jameson," said Judy, shaking a reproachful finger at him, "I believe you are afraid of your butler."

"Well, perhaps I am, my dear," said the Judge, weakly, "but Perkins is an individual of a great deal of firmness, and he carries the keys, and I don't believe you will find anything, anyhow. And if you eat up anything that he has ordered for breakfast, you will have an unpleasant time accounting for it in the morning. I know Perkins, my dear - and he is rather difficult - rather difficult. But he is a very fine servant," he amended hastily.

"You leave him to me in the morning," said Judy, "I'll make the peace, grandfather, and I simply can't be starved to-night."

"But Perkins -"

"Perkins won't say a word to you," said Judy, "and if he does, you can say you were not in the kitchen, because you are to stay right here, and Anne and I will bring things up, and make you a receiver of stolen goods."

She was very charming in spite of her wilfulness, and when she ended her little speech, by tucking her hand through the Judge's arm, and looking up at him mischievously, the old gentleman gave in.

The two girls were gone for a long time, so long that the Judge nodded on his bench.

He was waked by a shriek that seemed to come from the depths of the earth.

"What - is the matter, what's the matter, my dear?" he cried, starting up.

There was another subdued shriek, then a hysterical giggle.

"Judy is shut up in the ice-box," announced Anne, hurrying up from the basement.

"Bless my soul," ejaculated the Judge.

"We hunted around and found the key," explained Anne, as the Judge stumped distractedly through the lower hall, "and Judy unlocked the door of the ice-box and got inside, and she still had the key in her hand, and I hit the door accidentally and it slammed on her, and it has a spring lock and we can't open it."

"Bless my soul," said the Judge again.

The ice-box was a massive affair, almost like a small room. It was in a remote corner of the lower hallway, and its walls were thick and impenetrable.

"Let me out, oh, let me out," came in muffled tones, as the Judge and Anne came up.

"My dear child, my dear child," said the Judge, "how could you do such a thing?"

"I shall freeze. I shall freeze," wailed Judy.

"Are you very cold, Judy?" shivered Anne, sympathetically.

"It's so dark - and damp. Let me out, let me out," and Judy's voice rose to a shriek.

"Now, my dear, be calm," advised the Judge, whose hands were shaking with nervousness, "I shall call Perkins - yes, I really think I shall have to call Perkins -" and he hurried through the hall to the speaking tubes.

"Is there anything to eat in there?" Anne asked through the keyhole.

"Lots of things," said Judy. "I lighted a match as I came in, and there are lots of things. But I don't want anything to eat - I want to get out - I want to get out."

"Don't cry, Judy," advised Anne soothingly, "the Judge has called Perkins and he is coming down now."

Perkins emerged into the light of the lower hallway in a state of informal attire and unsettled temper. His dignity was his stock in trade, and how could one be dignified in an old overcoat and bedroom slippers? But the Judge's summons had been peremptory and there had been no time for the niceties of toilet in which Perkins' orderly soul revelled.

"There ain't no other key," he said, severely. "I guess we will have to wait until mornin', sir."

"But we can't wait until morning," raged the Judge, "the young lady will freeze."

"Oh, no, sir," said Perkins, loftily, "oh, no, sir, she won't freeze. Nothing freezes in that there box, sir."

"Well, she will die of cold," said the Judge. "Don't be a blockhead, Perkins, we have got to get her out now - at once - Perkins."

"All right, sir," said Perkins, "then I'll have to go for a

locksmith, sir -"

"Can't you take off the lock?" asked the Judge.

Perkins drew himself up. "That's not my work, sir," he said, stiffly, "no, sir, I can't take off no locks, sir," and so the Judge had to be content, while the independent Perkins hunted up a locksmith and brought him to the scene of disaster.

It was a white and somewhat cowed Judy that came out of the ice-box.

"Make her a cup of strong coffee, Perkins," commanded the Judge, as he received the woebegone heroine in his arms, "and take it up to her room, with something to eat with it."

"I don't want anything to eat," Judy declared. "There's everything to eat in that awful box - enough for an army - but I don't feel as if I could ever eat again," in a tone of martyr-like dolefulness.

"Them things in there is for the picnic, miss," said Perkins. "It's lucky you and Miss Anne didn't eat them," and he cast on the culprit a look of utter condemnation.

At the word "picnic," Anne's soul sank within her. She had forgotten all about the picnic in the excitement of the evening, all about Judy's anger and the confession she was to make of the plans for Saturday.

She and the Judge eyed each other guiltily, as Judy sank down on the bench and stared at Perkins.

"What picnic?" she demanded fiercely.

"The Judge said I was to get things ready, miss," said Perkins, dismally, and looked to his master for corroboration.

"Didn't you tell her, Anne?" asked the Judge, helplessly.

Anne felt as if she were alone in the world. Perkins and the Judge and Judy were all looking at her, and the truth had to come.

"We decided to have the picnic to-morrow, anyhow, Judy," she said. "We thought maybe you would like it after it was all planned."

Judy jumped up from the bench and began a rapid ascent of the stairway. Half-way up she turned and looked down at the three conspirators. "I sha'n't like it," she cried, shrilly, "and I sha'n't go."

"Judy!" remonstrated the Judge.

"Oh, Judy," cried poor little Anne.

But Perkins, who had lived with the Judge in the days of Judy's lady grandmother, turned his offended back on this self-willed and unworthy scion of a noble race, and marched into the kitchen to make the coffee.

CHAPTER IV

"YOUR GRANDMOTHER, MY DEAR"

Judy had reached the door of her room when the Judge called her.

"Come down," he said, "I want to talk to you."

"I'm tired," said Judy, in a stifled voice, and Anne, who had followed her, saw that she was crying.

"I know," the Judge's voice was gentle, "I know, but I won't keep you long. Come."

Judy went reluctantly, and he led the way to the garden bench.

It was very still out there in the garden - just the splash of the little fountain, and the drone of lazy insects. The moon hung low, a golden disk above the distant line of dark hills.

"Judy," began the Judge, "do you know, my dear, that you are very like your grandmother?"

Judy looked at him, surprised at the turn the conversation was taking. "Am I?" she asked.

"Yes," continued the Judge, "and especially in two things." His eyes were fixed dreamily on a bed of tall lilies that shone pale in the half light.

"What things?" Judy was interested. She had expected a lecture, but this did not sound like one.

"In your love of flowers - and in your temper - my dear."

Judy's head went up haughtily. "Grandfather!"

"You don't probably call it temper. But your grandmother did, and she conquered hers - and I am going to tell you how she did it, because I know she would want me to tell you, Judy."

Judy sat sulkily as far from her grandfather as she could get. Her hands were clasped around her knees and she stared out over the dusky garden, wide-eyed, and it must be confessed a little obstinate. Judy knew she had faults, but if the truth must be told, she was a little proud of her temper - "I have an awful temper," she had confessed on several occasions, and when meek admirers had murmured, "How dreadful," she had tossed her head and had said, "But I can't help it, you know, all of my family have had tempers," and as Judy's family was known to be aristocratic and exclusive, her more plebeian friends had envied and had tried to emulate her, generally with disastrous results.

She was not quite sure that she wanted to conquer it. It often gave her what she wanted, and that was something.

"The first time I had a taste of your grandmother's temper," the Judge related, "we had had an argument about a gown. We had been invited to a great dinner at the Governor's, and she had nothing to wear. She took me to the shop to see the stuff she wanted. It was heavy blue satin with pink roses all over it, and there was real lace to trim it with. It was beautiful and I wanted her to have it, but when they named the price it was more than I could pay - I was a poor lawyer in those days, Judy - so I said we would think it over, and we went home. All the way there your grandmother was very quiet and very white, but when we reached home and I tried to explain, she simply would not listen. She would not go to the Governor's, she said, unless she could have that gown. You can imagine the embarrassment it caused me - it was as much as my career was worth to stay away from that dinner, and I couldn't go without her.

"'I won't go. I won't go,' she said over and over again, and when I had coaxed and coaxed to no effect, I sat down and looked at her helplessly, and troubled as I was, I could not help thinking that she was the loveliest creature in the world - with her rose red cheeks and her flashing eyes.

"She said many cutting things to me, but suddenly she stopped and ran out of the room, and presently I saw her in the garden, this garden, my dear, and she was flying around the oval path, as if she were walking for a wager, her thin ruffles swirling around her, and the strings of her bonnet fluttering in the wind.

"Around and around she went, and I just sat there and stared. When she started in there was a deep frown on her forehead, but as she walked I saw her face clear, and when she had completed the round a dozen times or more, I saw her throw back her head in a light-hearted way, and then she ran into the house.

"She came straight to me and threw her arms around my neck. 'John,' she said, 'John, dear,' and there was the tenderest tremble in her voice, 'John Jameson, I was a hateful thing.' I tried to stop her, but she insisted. 'Oh, yes, I was. And I don't want the dress, I will wear an old one - and I'll make you proud of me -'

"Then all at once she began to sob, and her head dropped on my shoulder. 'Oh,' she cried, 'how could I say such things to you - how could I -?'

"'What made you change, sweetheart?' I asked, and she whispered, 'Oh, your face and the trouble in it.'

"'I made up my mind that I wouldn't say another word until I could get control of my temper, and so I went into the garden and walked and walked, and do you know, John Jameson, that I walked around that oval sixteen times before I could give up that dress.'

"It wasn't the last time she walked around that oval, Judy," the Judge finished, with a reminiscent smile on his old face, "and so perfectly did she conquer herself, that when she left me, it was just an angel stepping from earth to the place where she belonged."

Judy had listened breathlessly. So vivid had been the description, that she had seemed to see on the garden walk, the slender, imperious figure, the intent girlish face, and out of her knowledge of her own nature, she had entered into the struggle that had taken place in her grandmother's heart, as she flew around the oval of the old garden.

"Oh, grandfather," she said, when the Judge's quavering voice dropped into silence, "how lovely she was -"

"She was, indeed, and I want you to be as strong."

Judy tucked her hand into his. "I'll try," she said, simply, "thank you for telling me, grandfather."

"I want you to be happy here, too," said the old man wistfully, and then as she did not answer, "do you think you can, Judy?"

Judy caught her breath quickly. With all her faults she was very honest.

She bent and kissed the Judge on his withered cheek. "You are so good to me," she said, evasively, and with another kiss, she ran up-stairs to Anne.

Anne was in bed and Judy thought she was asleep, but an hour later as she lay awake lonely and restless, with her eyes fixed longingly on the great picture of the sea, a soft seeking hand curled within her own, and Anne whispered, "I didn't mean to make you unhappy, Judy," and Judy, clear-eyed and repentant in the darkness of the night, murmured back, "I was hateful, Anne," and a half hour later, the moon, peeping in, saw the two serene, sleeping faces, cheek to cheek on the same pillow.

Temple Bailey

CHAPTER V

TOO MANY COOKS

In spite of herself Judy was having a good time.

"I know you will enjoy it," had been Anne's last drowsy remark, and Judy's final thought had been, "I'll go, but it will be horrid."

But it wasn't horrid.

There had been Anne's happiness in the first place. Judy had wondered at it until she found out that Anne's picnic experiences had been limited to little jaunts with the children of the neighborhood, and an occasional Sunday-school gathering. The Judge had lived his lonely life in his lonely house, and except when Anne and her little grandmother had been invited to formal meals, he had not interested himself in any festivities.

There had been the early start, the meeting of the queer boy at the crossroads - the boy with the lazy air and the alert eyes; the crowding of the big carriage with two rather dowdy little country girls, one of whom was, in Judy's opinion, exceedingly pert, and the other exasperatingly placid; the laughter and the light-heartedness, the beauty of the blossoming spring world, the restfulness of the dim forest aisles, the excitement of the arrival on the banks of the stream, and the arrangement of the camp for the day.

And now Judy, having declined more active occupation, was in a hammock, swung in a circle of pines. The softened sunlight shone gold on the dried needles under foot, and everywhere was the aromatic fragrance of the forest. Now and then there was a flutter of wings as a nesting bird swooped by with scarcely a note of song. A pair of redbirds came and went - flashes of scarlet against the whiteness of a blossoming dogwood-tree. Far away the squalling of a catbird mingled with the mellow cadences of the mountain stream.

There was the sound of laughter, too, and the chatter of gay voices in the distance, where the young people fished from the banks.

Judy could just see them through an opening in the pines. The three girls perched on the bent trunk of an old tree, which hung over the water, were dangling their lines and watching the corks that bobbed on the surface. The Judge, with a big hat pushed away from his warm, red face, held the can of bait and discoursed entertainingly on his past angling experiences.

Perkins in the foreground was opening the lunch-hampers, and just outside of Judy's circle of pines, a brisk little fire sent up its pungent smoke, and beside the fire, Launcelot Bart was cutting bacon.

Judy watched him with interest. He was tall and thin, but he carried himself with a lazy grace, and in spite of his old corduroy suit, there was about him a certain air of distinction.

He was whistling softly as he put the iron pan over the coals, and dropped into it a half-dozen slices of the bacon.

"Watch these, Perkins," he called, "I'll be back in a minute," and he started towards the hammock.

As he came up, Judy closed her eyes, with an air of indifference.

"Asleep?" asked Launcelot, a half-dozen steps from her.

Judy opened her eyes.

"Oh - is that you?" she asked.

"Yes. Don't you want to come and help me cook?" He was smiling down at her pleasantly.

"I hate cooking." Judy's voice was cold. She hoped he would go away.

Launcelot leaned against a tree to discuss the question.

"Oh," he said. "I don't hate it. It's rather a fine art, you know."

"Anybody can cook," murmured Judy with decision.

"H-m. Can you, little girl?"

Judy sat up at that. "I'm fourteen," she flashed.

Launcelot laughed, such a contagious laugh, that in spite of herself Judy felt the corners of her lips twitch.

"That waked you up," he said, "you didn't like to have me call you 'little girl.' Well, am I to say Miss Jameson or Judy?"

Judy pondered.

"Neither," she said at last.

"Then what -?" began Launcelot. "Oh, by Jove, the bacon's burning. I'll be back in a minute."

When he had taken the bacon out of the pan, and had laid the fish in a corn-mealed symmetrical row in the hot fat, he again turned the pan over to Perkins and came back to Judy.

"Well?" he asked, as he came up.

"Call me Judith," said the incensed young lady. "Judy is my pet name, and I keep it for - my friends."

Launcelot gave a long whistle.

"Say, do you talk like this to Anne?" he asked.

"Like what?"

"In this - er - straight from the shoulder sort of fashion?"

"No. Anne is my friend."

Launcelot shook his head. "You can't have Anne for a friend unless you have me."

"Why not?"

"She was my friend first."

"Oh, well," Judy shrugged her shoulders and shut her eyes again, "it is too hot to argue."

There was a long silence, and then Launcelot said: "Don't you want to fish?"

"I hate fishing."

"Or to pick wild flowers?"

"I hate -" Judy had started her usual ungracious formula, before she recognized its untruth. "Well, I don't want to pick them now," she amended, "I'd rather stay here."

"But you are not going to stay here."

"Why not?"

"You are going to help me cook those fish."

"I won't."

"Oh, yes you will. Come on."

"Oh, well. If you won't let me alone."

She slipped out of the hammock and picked up her hat. There was a tired droop to her slender young figure. "No, I am not going to let you alone," said Launcelot quietly. "You poor little thing."

She looked at him, startled.

"Why?" she breathed.

"You are lonely. That's why. You've got to do something. You just think and think and think - and get miserable - I know - I've been there."

It came out haltingly, the boyish expression of sympathy and understanding. And the sympathy combined with a hitherto unmet masterfulness conquered Judy. For a moment she stood very still, then she turned to him an illumined face.

"You may call me - Judy," she said shyly, then slipped past him and ran to the fire.

When he reached her, she was bending over the pan.

"How nice they look," she said, as Launcelot turned the fish, and they lay all crisp and brown in an appetizing row.

"You shall do the next," said Launcelot, smiling a little as he glanced at her absorbed face.

So while he made the coffee, Judy fried more bacon, and they slipped six fish into the big pan.

"Mine don't seem to brown as yours did," she told him, anxiously.

"Perhaps the fat wasn't hot enough," was Launcelot's suggestion. "It has to be smoking."

"Oh, dear," sighed Judy, "mine are going to look light brown instead of lovely and golden like yours."

"Put on some more wood." Launcelot's tone was abstracted. He was measuring the coffee, and it took all of his attention.

Judy poked a stick into the centre of the fire. For a moment it seemed to die down, then suddenly the big black pan seemed held aloft by a solid cone of yellow flame.

The grease in the pan snapped, and little burnt bits of corn-meal flew in all directions.

"Now they are cooking all right," and Judy shielded her face with her hand, as she held the long handle and watched complacently.

Suddenly Launcelot dropped the coffee-pot.

"Take them off, take them off," he cried.

Judy, with her fork upraised, stared at him as if petrified.

"Why?" she stammered.

He snatched the pan from the fire.

"They're burning," he cried, and turned the fish up one by one.

They were as black as coals down to the very tips of their crisp little tails!

CHAPTER VI

A RAIN AND A RUNAWAY

At her cry of dismay, Perkins strolled over to take a look.

"They're burnt, Miss," he announced, bending over the pan.

"Of course they are," snapped Judy, "any one could see that, Perkins."

Perkins looked over her head, loftily.

"Yes, Miss, of course," he said, "but it's mostly always that way when there are too many cooks. I'm afraid there won't be enough to go around, Miss."

"Are these all?" asked Judy, anxiously.

"Yes," said Launcelot, "I cooked four and you burned six, and there are the Judge and Anne and Nannie and Amelia and Perkins and you and I to be fed."

"You needn't count me, sir," said Perkins. "I never eats, sir."

With which astounding statement, he carried away the charred remains.

"Does he mean that he doesn't eat at all?" questioned Judy, staring after the stout figure of the retiring butler.

Launcelot laughed. "Oh, he eats enough," he said, "only he doesn't do it in public. He knows his place."

"I wish he did," said Judy, dubiously. "Oh, dear, what shall we do about the fish?"

"There will be one apiece for the others," said Launcelot. "I guess you and I will have to do without - Judy -"

He spoke her name with just the slightest hesitation, and his eyes laughed as they met hers.

"And I said any one could cook!" Judy's tone was very humble. "What a prig you must have thought me, Launcelot."

"Oh, go and get some flowers for the table and forget your troubles," was Launcelot's off-hand way of settling the question, and as Judy went off she decided that she should like him. He was different from other boys. He was a gentleman in spite of his shabby clothes, and his masterfulness rather pleased her - hitherto Judy had ruled every boy within her domain, and Launcelot was a new experience.

It was a hungry crowd that trooped to the great gray rock where the table was spread.

"How beautiful you have made it look, Judy," cried Anne, as she came up, blissfully unconscious of a half-dozen new freckles and a burned nose.

Nannie May sniffed. "Fish," she said, ecstatically, "our fish, oh, Amelia, don't things look *good.*"

Amelia surveyed the table solemnly. She was a fat, rather dumpy girl of twelve. She was noted principally for two things, her indolence and her appetite, and it was in deference to the latter that she sighed rapturously as she surveyed the table. She had never seen anything just like it. The country picnics of the neighbors always showed an amazing array of cakes and pies and chicken, but these were here, and added to them were sandwiches of wonderful and attractive shapes, marvelous fruits, bonbons, and chocolates, and salads garnished with a skill known to none other in the village but the accomplished Perkins.

As her eyes swept over the table, they were arrested by the platter of fish. In spite of Perkins' overplentiful border of cress and sliced lemon - put on to hide deficiencies, the four fish looked pitifully inadequate.

"I caught four myself," said Amelia, heavily, pointing an accusing finger at the platter, "and Anne caught three and Nan three - there were ten."

Launcelot groaned. "I wish you weren't quite so good at arithmetic, Amelia," he said, "we shall have to confess - we burned the rest up - and please ma'am, we are awfully sorry."

They all laughed at the funny figure he made as he dropped on his knees before the stolid Amelia - but into Judy's cheeks crept a little flush - "I -" she began, with a tremble in her voice; but Launcelot interrupted; "we will never do it again," he promised, and then as they laughed again, he rose and stood at Judy's side.

"Don't you dare tell them that you did it," he whispered, and once more she felt the masterfulness of his tone. "I should have watched the fire - it was as much my fault as yours," and with that he picked up a pile of cushions, and went to arrange a place for her at the head of the table.

Amelia ate steadily through the menu. She was not overawed by Perkins, nor was her attention distracted by the laughter and fun of the others. It was not until the ice-cream was served - pink and luscious, with a wreath of rosy strawberries encircling each plate - that she spoke.

"Well," she said, "I don't know's I mind now about those fish being burned," with which oracular remark, she helped herself to two slices of cake, and ate up her ice in silence.

Nannie May was thirteen and looked about eleven. She was red-haired and fiery-tempered, and she loved Anne with all the strength of her loyal heart. As yet she did not like Judy. It was all very well to look like a princess, but that was no reason why one should be as stiff as a poker. She hoped Anne would not love Judy better than she did her, and she noted jealously the rapt attention with which Anne observed the newcomer and listened to all she said.

Judy was telling the episode of the ice-box. She told it well, and in spite of herself Nannie had to laugh.

"When I went in there were salads to right of me, cold tongue to the left of me, and roast chicken in front of me," said Judy, gesticulating dramatically, "and I was so hungry that it seemed too good to be true that Perkins should have provided all of those things. And just then the door slammed and my match went out - and there I was in the cold and the dark - and I just screamed for Anne."

"Why didn't you put the latch up when you went in?" asked Nannie, scornfully. "It seems to me 'most anybody would have thought of that."

Anne came eagerly to her friend's defence.

"Neither of us knew it was a spring latch," she said, "and I was as surprised as Judy was."

"Why didn't you eat up all the things?" asked Amelia, as she helped herself to another chocolate.

"I didn't have any light - " began Judy.

"Well, I should have eaten them up in the dark," mused Amelia, as Perkins passed her the salted almonds for the sixth time.

"It was a good thing I didn't," laughed Judy, "or you wouldn't have had anything to eat to-day. Would they, Perkins?"

For once in his life Perkins was in an affable mood. The lunch had gone off well, there had been no spiders in the cream or red ants in the cake. The coffee had been hot and the salads cold, and now that lunch was over he could pack the dishes away to be washed by the servants at home, and rest on his laurels.

"I should have found something, Miss," he said, cheerfully; then as a big drop splashed down on his bald head, he leaned over the Judge.

"I think it is going to rain, sir," he murmured, confidentially.

"By George," gasped the Judge, as a bright flash of light and a low rumble emphasized Perkins' words, "by George, I believe it is.

"Oh, oh, oh," screamed Amelia, and threw her arms frantically around Nannie.

"Don't be silly," said Nannie, and gave her a little shake.

"We shall have to run for it," said Launcelot, gathering up wraps and hats, as a sudden gust of wind picked up the ends of the tablecloth and sent the napkins fluttering across the ground like a flock of white geese.

"You'd better get the young ladies to the carriage, sir," said Perkins, packing things into hampers in a hurry.

"They will get wet. It's going to be a heavy wind storm," said the Judge with an anxious look at Judy.

"Let's run for the Cutter barn," cried Anne, with sudden inspiration.

"Good for you, Anne," said Launcelot, "that's the very thing."

"Where is the Cutter barn?" asked Judy.

"Across that stream and beyond the strip of woods. Over in the field."

"Come on, Anne, come on. Oh, isn't this glorious. I love the wind. I love it, I love it." Judy's cry became almost a chant as she led the way across the little bridge and through the fast-darkening bit of woodland. The wind fluttered her white garments around her, her long hair streamed out behind, and her flying feet seemed scarcely to touch the ground.

Behind her came Anne, less like a wood-nymph, perhaps, but fresh and fair, and not at all breathless, then Nannie, bare-headed and with her best hat wrapped carefully in her short skirts, then Amelia, plunging heavily.

Launcelot waited to help Perkins with the horses and hampers and then he followed the girls.

The rain came before he was half-way across the stream, and the world grew dark for a moment in the heavy downpour that drenched him. There was a blaze of blue-white light, and a crash that seemed to shake the universe.

"They will be scared half to death," was Launcelot's thought as he forged ahead.

Just at the edge of the woods he came upon Anne and Judy. Judy had dropped down in a white huddled bunch, and Anne was bending over her.

"She ran too fast," she explained, while the rain beat down on her fair little head, "and she can't get her breath. Nannie and Amelia got to the barn before the rain came, but I couldn't leave Judy."

"I'm all right," gasped Judy, "you run on, Anne. I'm all right."

"Yes, run on, Anne," commanded Launcelot. "I'll take care of Judy, and you must not get wet," and with a protest Anne disappeared behind the curtain of driving rain.

Judy staggered to her feet and attempted to walk two or three steps.

"Stop it," said Launcelot, firmly, "you must not."

"But I can't stay here," cried poor Judy, desperately.

Her lips were blue and her cheeks were white, so that Launcelot wavered no longer. Without any warning, he picked her up as if she had been a child, and ran with her across the field.

"Put me down, Launcelot. Put me down." Judy's tone was imperious.

But she had met her match. Launcelot plodded on doggedly.

"I shall never forgive you," she sobbed, as they reached the door of the Cutter barn.

"Yes, you will," said Launcelot, and his lips were set in a firm line. "I had to do it, Judy."

He laid her on a pile of hay in the corner.

Her eyes were closed, and her dark lashes swept across her pallid cheeks.

"She isn't strong," whispered the worried Anne, her tender fingers pushing back Judy's wet hair.

"No," said Launcelot, his deep young voice softening to a gentler key as he looked down at her, "she isn't. Poor little thing!"

Judy heard, and her lashes fluttered. "How good they are," she thought, remorsefully, and then she seemed to float away from realities.

When she came to herself, Launcelot had gone, and the three little girls were rubbing her hands and trying to get her to drink some water.

"Oh, Judy, do you feel better?" Anne whispered; "we were so frightened."

"Yes," murmured Judy, and the color began to come into her face.

"Launcelot went to see if he could get something from Perkins for you to take," said Anne; "he told us to build a fire in the old stove, but we have been so worried about you that we haven't done anything."

"Is there a stove?" asked Judy, listlessly.

"Yes. Mr. Cutter put it in here to heat milk for the lambs, and once when we had a picnic we made our coffee here."

"There isn't any wood," said Amelia, hopelessly.

"There is some up in the loft," said Nannie, "Don't you remember the boys put it there, so that no one but ourselves could find it?"

She went swiftly up the narrow steps, but came flying back in a panic.

"*There's some one up there*," she whispered, all the color gone from her face.

"Hush," said Anne, with her eyes on Judy.

Judy was not afraid. She was still weak and wan, but she was braver than the little country girls, and not easily frightened.

"It is probably a pussy cat," she scoffed.

"Or a hen," giggled Amelia.

Anne said nothing. The darkness, the crashing storm outside, and Judy's illness had upset her, and she shivered with apprehension.

"No," Nannie flared, with a scornful look at Amelia and Judy, "it isn't a cat and it isn't a hen. IT sneezed!"

"Ask who's there," advised Judy from her couch.

"I don't dare," said Nannie.

"I don't dare," said Amelia.

So that it was little timid Anne, after all, who gathered up her courage and went to the foot of the stairs and said in a trembling voice:

"Please, who is up there?"

For a moment there was silence, and then some one said in sepulchral tones:

"You won't ever tell?"

The girls stared at each other.

"What shall we say?" whispered Anne.

"Say 'never,'" suggested Judy, wishing she were well enough to manage this exciting episode.

"NEVER," said the little girls all together.

There was a rustling in the hay in the loft, then cautious steps, and a figure appeared at the top of the stairs.

At sight of it, Amelia shrieked and Nannie giggled, but Anne ran forward with both hands out, and with her fair little face alight with welcome.

"Why, Tommy Tolliver, Tommy Tolliver," she said, "is it really you, is it really, really you?"

CHAPTER VII

TOMMY TOLLIVER: SEAMAN

Tommy shook hands with Anne, then sat down disconsolately on the bottom step.

"Yes," he said, "it's me."

After a moment's uncomfortable silence, Anne asked, "Didn't you like it, Tommy?"

Tommy looked gloomy.

"Aw," he burst out, "they thought I was too young -"

"Did you go as far as China?" questioned Amelia, eagerly.

"Of course he didn't, Amelia," said Nannie with a superior air; "he has only been away three weeks."

"Then you didn't get me any preserved ginger," pouted Amelia.

"How could I?" But Tommy looked sheepish, as the memory of certain boastful promises came to him.

"Anyhow," he announced suddenly, "I'm not going to give up. I am going to be a sailor some day - if I have to run away again."

At that Judy sat up and fixed him with burning eyes.

"Did you go to sea?" she asked, intensely.

"I tried to."

"How far did you get?"

"To Baltimore."

"And they wouldn't have you?"

"No. And I had used up all my money, so I had to come back."

"Have you ever been on the ocean?"

"No. Have you?"

"Yes. My father was in the navy."

"Gee -" Tommy drew near to this fascinating stranger.

"The next time you want to run away, you tell me," said Judy, and sank back on the hay, "and I'll help you."

"But, Judy," said horrified little Anne, "he isn't going to run away any more - he is going to stay here, and please his father and go to school - aren't you, Tommy?"

Tommy looked from the fair little girl to the dark thin one. Hitherto Anne had been his ideal of gentle girlhood, but in Judy he now found a kindred spirit, a girl with a daring that more than matched his own - a girl who loved the sea - who knew about the sea - who could tell him things.

"Aw - I don't know," he said, uncertainly. "I guess I can run away if I want to, Anne."

"No, you can't," cried Anne. "You ought not to encourage him, Judy."

"I'm not encouraging him," said Judy, but there was a wicked sparkle in her eyes.

Tommy saw it and swaggered a little. He had returned home in the spirit of the prodigal son. He was ready to be forgiven. To eat of the fatted calf - if he should be so lucky. If not, to eat humble pie. The sight of the familiar fields and roads had even brought tears to his eyes. But now -!

"A fellow can't be tied to a little old place like this all his life," he said, toploftically, "you can't expect it, Anne."

"I don't expect it," said little Anne, quietly, "but if you had seen your mother after you ran away, Tommy -"

At that Tommy lowered his head.

"I know -" he stammered, huskily, "poor little mother."

"Tell me about her," he said. And now he turned his back on the dark young lady on the hay.

But Launcelot's voice broke in on Anne's story. He came in all wet and dripping.

"How's Judy?" he began, then stopped and whistled.

"Hello," he exclaimed, "hello, Bobby Shafto."

"Oh, I say," said Tommy, very red.

"I thought you were on the high seas by now," said Launcelot.

"Well, I wanted to be," said Tommy, resentfully.

"I am glad you're back. We have missed you awfully, old chap," and Launcelot slapped him on the shoulder in hearty greeting.

"How is Judy?" he asked.

"Better, thank you," said the young lady in the corner. "Tommy was a tonic and came just in time."

"Well, I am glad you found some kind of tonic. Perkins didn't have a thing but some mustard and red pepper, and I was feeling for you if we had to dose you with either of those."

Judy started to laugh, but stopped suddenly.

"I forgot," she said, "I am mad at you -"

"Oh, no, you're not."

"But I am -"

"Because I carried you across the field when you didn't want me to?"

"Yes."

"My child," advised Launcelot, "don't be silly."

"Oh," raged Judy, and turned her back to him.

Launcelot looked down at her for a moment.

"You know that tree where you fainted?" he asked.

A little shrug of Judy's shoulder was the only answer.

"Well, it was struck by lightning before I got back -"

"Really - ?" Judy was facing him now, breathless with interest.

"Really, Judy." His face was very grave.

"Oh, oh," she wailed, softly, "oh, and I might have been there -"

"Yes."

She shivered and sat up. Her wet hair, half braided, trailed its dark length over her shoulder. Her eyes were big, and her face was white.

"What a baby I was," she said, nervously, "what a baby, Launcelot - not to see the danger -"

"You trust to your Uncle Launcelot, next time, little girl, and don't get fussy," was the big boy's way of stopping her thanks.

"I will," she promised, and the smile she gave him meant more than the words.

"It has stopped raining," said Anne from the door.

The cool spring air blew across the fields softly, bringing with it the fresh smell of the sodden earth and the scent of the wet pines.

"The Judge will be here in a minute," said Launcelot; "he stayed in the carriage, and Perkins put up the curtains, so that they managed to keep pretty dry."

"I wonder if there will be room for me to ride home?" Tommy asked. "I am dead tired."

"I guess so. The Judge has the big wagon with the three seats. Pretty long tramp you had, didn't you?" and Launcelot looked at the boy's dusty shoes.

"Awful," said Tommy, with a quiver in his voice at the remembrance.

"Hungry?" questioned Launcelot, briefly.

"Awful," said Tommy again. "I haven't had a square meal for a week," and now the quiver was intensified.

Amelia clasped her hands tragically. "Oh, Tommy," she asked in a stricken tone, "didn't you almost die?"

But just then Tommy caught Judy's eye on him, and was forced to continue his character of bold adventurer.

"Oh, a man must expect things like that," he asserted. "Suppose it had been a desert island -"

"Or a shipwreck," said Amelia, "with bread and water for a week."

"Or pirates," ventured Nannie.

"Oh, pirates," sniffed the dark young lady on the hay; "there aren't any pirates now."

"Well, there are shipwrecks," defended Tommy.

"Yes, but they are not half as interesting as they used to be."

"And desert islands."

"A few maybe. But it is such an old story to hear about Robinson Crusoes."

Tommy looked blank. He had always implicitly believed the marvelous tales of yarn spinners, and his soul had been fired by the thought of a life of adventure on the deep. He had talked to the little girls until they had accounted him somewhat of a hero and looked to him to perform great feats of bravery.

"I don't see any fun in going to sea, then," he said, dolefully, "if there ain't any pirates and shipwrecks and things like that -"

"It isn't those things that make you love the sea, Tommy,"

cried Judy. "It is the smell of it, and the wind, and the wide blue water and the wide blue sky. It is something in your blood. I don't believe you really love it at all, Tommy Tolliver."

She got up from the couch and began to gather up her wet hair, and only Launcelot saw that she did it to hide her tears.

But Tommy was blind to her emotion. "Yes, I do," he asserted, stoutly. "I do love it, and I bet I could find a treasure island if I tried."

Judy stamped her foot impatiently. "Oh, you couldn't," she blazed, "you couldn't, Tommy Tolliver; you could just go to work like a common seaman and get your tobacco and your grog, and be frozen and stiff in the winter storms and hot and weary in the summer ones. But if you really loved the sea you wouldn't care - you wouldn't care, just so you could be rocked to sleep by it at night, and wake to hear it ripple against the sides of the boat -"

"Gee -" said Tommy, open-mouthed at this outburst.

"Tommy," said Launcelot, with a glance at Judy's excited face and at the trembling hands that could scarcely fasten her hair, "you don't know a sailboat from a scow."

"I do," cried the indignant Tommy, switching his attention from Judy to Launcelot, with whom he was deep in the argument when the carriage came.

The Judge read Tommy a little lecture as he welcomed him back, and then he ordered Perkins to give the runaway something to eat, and thereby tempered justice with mercy. And as Tommy had expected the scolding and had not expected the good things, it is to be feared that the latter made the greater impression.

"And how is my girl?" asked the Judge, beaming on Judy.

"All right," said Judy, and tucked her hand into his, "only I am a little tired, grandfather."

"Of course you are. Of course you are," said the Judge. "We must go right home. Perkins and I will sit on the front seat, and you can all crowd in behind - I guess there will be room enough."

"Oh, I say," said Launcelot, as Tommy and Anne sat down on the floor at the back, with their feet on the step, "that won't do. You sit with Judy, Anne."

But Anne shook her head.

"Tommy and I are going to sit here," she said. "He wants me to tell him all the news."

But that was not all that Tommy wanted, for when they were alone and unseen by those in the front of the wagon, he opened a handkerchief which he had carried knotted into a bundle.

"I brought you some things. They ain't much, but I thought you would like to have them."

There were a half-dozen pink and white shells, a starfish, and a few pretty pebbles.

"I picked them up on the beach," said Tommy, "and I thought you might like them."

"It was awfully good of you to think of me," said little Anne, gratefully.

"I wanted to buy you something," apologized Tommy. "There was some lovely jewelry made out of fish-scales, but I didn't have a cent to spare."

"I would rather have these, really, Tommy," said Anne, with

appreciation, "because you found them yourself."

She tied them up carefully in her little clean white hand-kerchief, and then she folded her hands in her lap and told Tommy everything that had happened since he left home.

The sky was red with the blaze of the setting sun when the carriage started. Overhead the crows were flying in a straight black line to the woods to roost. As Anne talked on, the fireflies began to shine against the blue-gray of the twilight; then came darkness and the stars.

"It seems awfully good to be at home," confessed Tommy, as the lights began to twinkle in the nearest farmhouse, "if only father won't scold."

"I think he will scold, Tommy - he was awfully angry - but your mother will be so pleased."

"It was horrid sleeping out at night and tramping days." Tommy was unburdening his soul. It was so easy to tell things to gentle, sympathetic Anne. "And the men around the wharf were so rough -"

"I am sure you won't want to go again," said little Anne, "not for a long time, Tommy."

Tommy looked around cautiously. He didn't want Judy to hear, somehow. He was afraid of her teasing laugh. Then he leaned down close to Anne's ear:

"I'll stay here for awhile, Anne."

"I'm so glad, Tommy," said Anne, with a sigh of relief.

But as they drove into the great gateway, and the lights from the big house shone out in welcome, Tommy sighed:

"But I would like to find a treasure island, Anne," he said.

CHAPTER VIII

A WHITE SUNDAY

Anne was feeling very important. She was wrapped in a pale blue kimona of Judy's, and she had had her breakfast in bed!

Piled up ten deep at her side were books - a choice collection from the Judge's bookcases, into which she dipped here and there with sighs of deep content and anticipation.

At the end of the room was a mirror, and Anne could just see herself in it. It was a distracting vision, for Judy had done Anne's hair up that morning, and had puffed it out over her ears and had tied it with broad black ribbon, and this effect, in combination with the sweeping blue robe, made Anne feel as interesting as the heroine of a book - and she had never expected that!

Judy in a rose-pink kimona lay on the couch, looking out of the window. The peace of the Sabbath was upon the world; and the house was very still.

Suddenly with a "click" and a "whirr-rr," the doors of the little carved clock on the wall new open and a cuckoo came out and piped ten warning notes.

"Goodness," cried Anne, and shut her book with a bang, "it is almost church time, and we aren't dressed."

Temple Bailey

But Judy did not move. "We are not going to church," she said, lazily.

Not going to church! Anne faced Judy in amazement. Never since she could remember had she stayed away from church - except when she had had the measles and the mumps!

"I told grandfather last night that we should be too tired," explained Judy, "and he won't expect us to go."

"Oh," said Anne, and picked up her book, luxuriating in the prospect of a whole morning in which to read.

She wasn't quite comfortable, however. She was not a bit tired, and she had never felt better in her life - and yet she was staying away from church.

But the book she had opened was a volume of Dickens' Christmas stories, and in three minutes she was carried away from the little town of Fairfax to the heart of old London, and from the warmth of spring to the bitterness of winter, as she listened with Toby Veck to the music of the chimes that rang from the belfry tower.

It seemed only a part of the tale, therefore, when the bell of Fairfax church pealed out the first warning of the Sunday service to all the countryside.

"Ding dong, din, all come in, all come in," the bell had said to Anne since childhood, and now it called her, until it silenced the crashing voices of the bells of old London, and she had to listen.

She laid down her book. "The church bell is ringing," she said to Judy.

"I hear it," said Judy, indifferently.

Anne stood up - with a sidelong glance at the enchanting

vision in the mirror. "I think I ought to go," she hesitated.

Judy turned to look at her.

"Don't be so good, Anne," she said, with a teasing laugh; "be wicked like I am, just for one day -"

"You are not wicked."

"Well, I haven't a proper sense of duty."

"You have too. You just like to say such things, Judy, just to shock people."

Which shows that in two days, wise little Anne had found Judy out!

"Well, I'm not going to church, anyhow," and Judy settled back and closed her eyes.

Anne's book was open at the fascinating place where Toby Veck eats his dinner on the church steps; the deep rose-cushioned chair opened its wide arms in comfortable invitation. It was the little girl's first taste of the temptation of ease, - and she yielded. But as she picked up her book again, she soothed her conscience with the righteous resolve - "I will go to service this afternoon."

As she settled back, the girl reflected in the mirror looked at her.

"Your hair looks beautiful," said the reflection.

Anne dropped her eyes to her book.

Presently she raised them.

"If only the people in church could see," said the charming reflection.

Anne imagined the sensation she would make as she walked up the aisle. None of the girls in Fairfax or the country around had ever worn their hair puffed over their ears or tied with broad black ribbon. There would be a little flutter, and during church time the girls would look at nothing else, and it would be delightful to feel that for once she, little plain Anne Batcheller, was the center of attraction.

She dropped her book. "I think I will go, after all," she said virtuously, and Judy, not knowing her motive, looked at her with envy.

"You are a good little thing, Anne," she said, and at the praise Anne's face flamed.

She dressed hurriedly, in her one white dress, with a sigh for the becomingness of the blue kimona. When she was ready to tie on her old hat, she went to the mirror.

"It is because your hair is so pretty that you are going to church," said the reflection, accusingly.

"It is because of my conscience," defended Anne, but she did not dare to meet the eyes in the mirror, and she turned away quickly.

"You look awfully nice," Judy assured her, as Anne said "Good-by." "Take my blue parasol. It is on the parlor sofa. Go and be good for both of us, Annekins."

Anne ran down-stairs to the great dim room. There were four mirrors in the parlor, and each mirror seemed to say to the little girl as she passed, "It is because of your hair," and when she had picked up the pretty parasol, the mirrors said again, as she passed them going back, "It is because of your hair, oh, Anne, it is because of your hair that you are going to church!"

The hands of the big clock in the hall were on eleven as Anne opened the front door - and as she stepped out into the glare of sunshine, the church bell rang for the last time.

Anne loved the sweet old bell. Even when she had been ill, she had been able to hear just the end of its distant peal - like the ringing of a fairy chime, and when she was very little, the time she had the mumps, she had thought of it as being up in the clouds, calling the angels to worship.

She listened to it for a moment, standing perfectly still on the path, then she went back into the house, and laid the parasol carefully on the sofa. After that she ran quickly upstairs, untying her hat-strings as she went.

"What in the world are you doing?" asked Judy in amazement, as Anne pulled out hairpins, and took the big black bow from her looped-up hair.

"I was thinking too much about it," said Anne, soberly. "I shouldn't have heard a word of the sermon if I had worn my hair that way," and she went on braiding it into its customary tight and unbecoming pigtails.

"Well, of all things," ejaculated Judy, gazing at her spellbound.

But when Anne had gone, Judy stood up and watched her from the window. "What a queer little thing she is," she murmured, as the bobbing figure went up and down the village path, "what a queer little thing she is."

But somehow the actions of the queer girl distracted her mind so that she could not go back to her attitude of lazy indifference. She had thought Anne a little commonplace until now; but it had not been a commonplace thing, that changing from prettiness to plainness. She even wondered if Anne had not done a finer act than she could have done herself.

"She is a queer little thing," she said again, thoughtfully, and after a long pause, "but she is good -"

She went to her wardrobe and took out a white dress. Then she got out her hat and gloves and laid them on the bed. And then she sat and looked at them, and then she began to dress.

And so it came about that Fairfax church had that morning two sensations. In the first place Anne Batcheller came in late for the only time in her life, and in the second place, when the service was half over, a slender, distinguished maiden in a violet-wreathed white hat, slipped along the aisle, flashing a glance at Anne as she passed, and smiling at the delighted Judge as she entered the pew.

She fixed her eyes on the minister - and straightway forgot Anne and the Judge and Fairfax, for the minister was reading the 107th Psalm, and the words that fell on Judy's ears were pregnant with meaning to this daughter of a sailor - "They that go down to the sea in ships -"

Dr. Grennell was a plain man, a man of rugged exterior - but he was a man of spiritual power - and he knew his subject. His father had been a sea-captain, and back of that were generations of Newfoundland fishermen - men who went out in the glory of the morning to be lost in the mists of the evening - men who worked while women wept - men to whom this Psalm had been the song of hope - women to whom it had been the song of comforting.

To Judy the sea meant her father. It had taken him away, it would bring him back some day, and was not this man saying it, as he ended his sermon, "He bringeth them into their desired haven - "?

Dr. Grennell had never seen Judy, but he knew the tragedy in the Judge's life, and as she listened to him, Judy's face told him who she was.

She went straight up to him after church.

"I am Judy Jameson," she said, "and I want to tell you how

much I liked the sermon."

The doctor looked down into her moved young face. "I am the son of a sailor," he said, "and I love the sea -"

"I love it -" she said, with a catch of her breath, "and it is not cruel - is it?"

"No -" he began. But with a man of his fiber the truth must out; "not always," he amended, and took her hands in his, "not always -"

"And men do come back," she said, eagerly; "the one you told about in your sermon -"

He saw the hope he had raised. "Yes, men do come back - but not always, Judy."

Her lip quivered. "Let me believe it," she pleaded, and in that moment, Judy's face foreshadowed the earnestness of the woman she was to be. "Let me believe that my father will come some day -"

"Indeed, I will," said the doctor, and there was a mist in his eyes as he clasped her hand, "and you must let me be your friend, Judith, as I was your father's."

"I shall be glad -" she said, simply, and then and there began a friendship that some day was to bring to Judy her greatest happiness.

That afternoon the Judge and Judy drove Anne home.

"It seems just like a dream," said Anne, as they came in sight of the little gray house, with Belinda chasing butterflies through the clover, and Becky Sharp on the lookout in the plumtree. "It seems just like a dream - the good times and all, since Friday, Judy."

"A good dream or a bad dream, Annekins?" asked Judy.

"Oh, a good one, a lovely dream, and you are the Princess in it, Judy," said the adoring Anne.

"Well, you are the good little fairy godmother," said Judy. "Isn't she good, grandfather?"

"Oh, I am not," said Anne, greatly embarrassed at this over-whelming praise, "I am not -"

"I never could have changed my hair," affirmed Judy.

"What's that?" asked the Judge.

"Oh, a little secret," said Judy, smiling. "Shall I tell him, Anne?"

"No, indeed," Anne got very red, "no, indeed, Judy Jameson."

There was a little pause, and then the Judge said:

"I am sorry the picnic was such a failure."

"Oh, but it wasn't," cried Judy, "it wasn't a failure."

Anne and the Judge stared at her. "Did you enjoy it, Judy?" they asked in one breath.

"Of course I did," said the calm young lady.

"But the rain," said the Judge.

"That was exciting."

"And your fainting -" said Anne.

"Just an episode," said Judy, wafting it away with a flirt of her finger-tips.

"And Amelia, and Nannie, and Tommy, did you like them?" asked Anne.

"Oh, Amelia is funny, and Nannie is clever, and Tommy is a curiosity. Oh, yes, I liked them," summed up Judy.

"And Launcelot -"

Judy smiled an inscrutable smile, as she pulled her hat low over her sparkling eyes.

"He's bossy," she began, slowly, "and we are sure to quarrel if we see much of each other - but he is interesting - and I think I shall like him, Anne."

And then Belinda and Becky discovered them, and made for their beloved mistress, and conversation on the picnic or any other topic was at an end.

CHAPTER IX

A BLUE MONDAY

There was a noisy scrambling in the vines outside of Anne's window early on Monday morning, and the little maid opened her eyes to see Belinda's white head peeping over the sill, and Belinda's white paws holding on like grim death to the ledge.

"You darling," cried Anne, sitting up, "come here," and Belinda with a plaintive mew made one last effort, pulled herself into the room, and flew to her mistress' arms.

"Where's Becky?" asked Anne, wondering why the tame crow did not follow, for in spite of their constant feuds, the two pets were inseparable.

Belinda blinked sagely, while from a shadowy corner of the room came a sepulchral croak.

"Are you there, Becky?" called Anne, peering into the darkness, and with a flap and a flutter, Becky swooped from the top of the bookcase, where she had been perched for a half-hour, waiting for Anne to wake.

Anne's bookcase was the one thing of value in the little house. It was of rich old mahogany, with diamond-shaped panes in its leaded doors, and behind the doors were books - not many of them, but very choice ones, culled from a fine library which had been sold when ruin came to Anne's grandfather and father one disastrous year.

It happened, therefore, that Anne had read much of poetry and history, and the lives of famous people, to say nothing of fairy-tales and legends, so that in the companionship of her books and pets, she had missed little in spite of her poverty and solitary life.

"How good it is to be at home," she said, as the sunlight, creeping around the room, shone on the green cover of a much-thumbed book of French fairy-tales, and then slanted off to touch the edge of a blue and gold Tennyson; "how good it is to be at home."

"How good it is to be at home," she said again, as followed by Belinda and Becky, she came, a half-hour later, into the sunlit kitchen, where the little grandmother, smiling and rosy, was pouring the steaming breakfast food into a blue bowl.

"I was afraid you might find it dull," said the little grandmother, as she kissed her, "after the good times at the Judge's."

"Oh, I did have such lovely times," sighed Anne, blissfully. She had sat up late in the moonlight the night before, telling her grandmother of them. "But they didn't make up for you and Becky and Belinda and the little gray house," and she hugged the little grandmother tightly while Belinda and Becky circled around them in great excitement, mingled with certain apprehensions for the waiting breakfast.

"But I do hate to start to school again," said Anne, when she finished breakfast, and had given Belinda a saucer of milk and Becky a generous piece of corn bread.

"Are the children going to speak their pieces this week?" asked Mrs. Batcheller, as Anne tied on her hat and went out into the garden to gather some roses for the teacher.

"Yes, on Saturday," said Anne; "it's going to be awfully nice. I have asked Launcelot and Judy to come to the entertainment, and they have promised to."

"I am going to be 'Cinderella' in the tableaux," she went on, as her grandmother brought out the tiny lunch-basket and handed it to her, "and Nannie and Amelia are to be the haughty sisters. We haven't found any boy yet for the prince. I wish Launcelot went to school."

"He knows all that Miss Mary could teach him now," said the little grandmother; "his father is preparing him for college, if they ever get money enough to send him there."

"Well, if Launcelot's violets sell as well next winter as they did this, he can go, 'specially if his mother keeps her boarders all summer. He told me so the other day, grandmother."

"But he would make a lovely prince," she sighed. "Judy is going to lend me a dress. She has a trunk full of fancy costumes."

"I hope you know your lessons," said the old lady, as Anne, escorted by her faithful pets, started off.

"Oh, I studied them on Friday, before Judy came - how long ago that seems -" and with a rapturous sigh in memory of her three happy days, and with a wave of her hand to the little grandmother, Anne went on her way.

Tommy Tolliver came to school that morning in a chastened spirit. He had been lectured by his father, and cried over by his mother, and in the darkness of the night he had resolved many things.

But it is not easy to preserve an attitude of humility when one becomes suddenly the center of adoring interest to twenty-five children in a district school. From the babies of the A, B, C, class to the big boys in algebra, Tommy's return was an exciting event, and he was received with acclaim.

Hence he boasted and swaggered for them as on Saturday he had boasted and swaggered for Judy's admiration.

"You ought to go," he was saying to a small boy, as Anne came up, but when he caught her reproachful eye on him, he backed down, "but not until you are a man, Jimmie," he temporized.

During the morning session he was a worry and an aggravation to Miss Mary. The little girls could look at nothing else, for had not Tommy been a sailor, and had he not had experiences which would set him apart from the commonplace boys of Fairfax? And the boys, a little jealous, perhaps, were yet burning with a desire to be the bosom friend of this bold, bad boy, while the luster of his daring lasted.

And so they were all restless and inattentive, until finally Miss Mary, who had a headache, lost patience.

"You are very noisy," she said, "and I am ashamed of you. I am going to put a list of words on the board, and I want you to copy them five times, while I take the little folks out into the yard for their recess. The rest of you don't deserve any, and will have to wait until noon."

That was the first piece of injustice to Anne. She had been as quiet as a mouse all the morning, and Miss Mary should have seen it and not have punished the innocent with the guilty. But Anne was a cheery little soul and never thought of questioning Miss Mary's mandates, and so she went on patiently writing with the rest.

Miss Mary stopped in the door long enough to issue an ultimatum.

"I shall put you on your honor," she said, "not to talk. And any one who disobeys will be punished."

And she went out.

Temple Bailey

For a little while there was perfect decorum. Then Tommy grew restless. Six weeks out of school had made sitting still almost impossible. He wiggled around in his seat, and began to whistle, "A Life on an Ocean Wave."

That was a signal for general disorder among the boys. Without speaking a word, and so preserving the letter of the rule, if not the spirit, they, with Tommy as leader, went through various pantomimic performances. They hitched up their trousers in seamanlike fashion, they pretended to row boats, they spit on their hands and hauled in imaginary ropes, and as a climax, Tommy danced a hornpipe on his toes.

And then Anne spoke right out - "Oh, Tommy, *don't*," she said, in an agony of fear lest Miss Mary should come in and catch him at it.

But Miss Mary did not come, and the little girls giggled and the boys capered, and Anne in despair went on writing her words.

When Miss Mary came back finally, with the little people trooping in a rosy row behind her, twenty-five virtuous heads were bent over twenty-five papers.

"Did any one speak while I was out?" asked the teacher.

A wave of horror swept over Anne. She had not meant to do it, but she had spoken, and to try to explain would be to condemn Tommy and the rest of the school.

"Did any one speak?" asked Miss Mary again.

Anne stood up, her face flaming.

"I - I - did -" she faltered.

"Oh, Anne -" said Miss Mary, while the girls and boys dropped their eyes for very shame. "Oh, Anne, why did you do it -"

"I just did it - " stammered Anne, who would rather have died than have blamed Tommy, and Nannie, and Amelia, and the rest of her friends.

"Well, then," said Miss Mary, firmly, "I'm sorry, but you will have to sit on the platform the rest of the morning, and I can't let you take part in the Saturday's entertainment. I must have order and I will have it."

And that was Miss Mary's second piece of injustice. But then she had a headache, and children on Monday mornings are troublesome.

For one hour Anne sat with her head held high and her fair little face flushed and burning. But she did not cry. And Tommy, bowed to the ground by his sense of guilt in the matter, did not dare to look at the patient, suffering martyr.

It was thus that Launcelot Bart, coming in just before twelve o'clock to see Tommy, found her.

As soon as he got Tommy outside of the schoolroom he collared him.

"What's the matter with Anne?" he demanded.

"She talked in school," said Tommy, doggedly.

"I don't believe it."

"Well, she did, anyhow."

"Whose fault was it?"

"Hers, I suppose."

"You don't suppose anything of the kind. Anne Batcheller never broke a rule in her life willingly, and you know it, Tommy Tolliver."

The children were coming out of the schoolroom in little groups of twos and threes - the girls discussing Anne's martyrdom sympathetically, the boys with hangdog self-consciousness.

Inside the room, Anne, released from her ordeal, had gone to her desk and was sitting there with her head up. Her face was white now, the little lunch-basket was open before her, but the cookie and the apple were untouched.

Launcelot looked in through the window.

"Poor little soul," he murmured.

And then Tommy blubbered.

"It was really my fault, Launcelot," he confessed.

"What!"

Tommy explained.

"And you let Anne bear it - you let Anne be punished - oh, you miserable - little - little - cur," said the indignant squire of dames, in a white heat.

"Aw, what could I do?" whimpered Tommy.

"Go in and tell Miss Mary," said Launcelot.

"Aw - Launcelot -"

"*Go in and tell Miss Mary!*"

Tommy went.

But Miss Mary did not wish to be bothered.

"I made a rule and Anne broke it," she said, when Tommy

tried to straighten things out, "and that is all there is to it. Don't talk about it any more, Tommy," and she dismissed him peremptorily.

When Tommy told Launcelot the result of the interview, the big boy set his lips in a firm line, and started off down the dusty road.

He went straight to town and to Judy.

"Oh, oh," said Judy, when she had listened to his tale of woe, "what a mean old thing she is - I hate her -" and her dark eyes flashed.

"I don't think Miss Mary is mean," said Launcelot, "but the children *are* restless, and she isn't very strong, and when she feels badly she takes it out on the scholars."

"But to punish Anne," said Judy, and her voice trembled, "dear little Anne -"

"She might at least have listened to Tommy's explanation," said Launcelot.

After a pause he said: "I came to you because I thought you might go and see Anne after school. It would do her a lot of good. She will be all broken up."

"I will go to school and get her," cried Judy, eagerly. "Is it very far?"

"I am afraid you couldn't walk," said Launcelot, doubtfully.

"I'll drive over in the trap," said Judy. "Grandfather says I can use Vic whenever I want to."

"It was pretty mean of Miss Mary to pile it on, I must say," said Launcelot, as he rose to go. "She might have let Anne be in the entertainment."

"What?"

"She isn't going to let Anne be in it."

"Not be 'Cinderella'?" Judy's tone was ominous.

"No."

"Oh, oh, oh." Judy's hands were clenched fiercely. "I'll get even with her, Launcelot. I'll get even with that teacher yet."

Launcelot smiled at her vehemence.

"But you can't," he said.

"Can't I?" with a shrug of her shoulders.

"No."

"Wait," said Judy, and not another word could he get out of her on the subject.

The afternoon dragged along its interminable length, and Anne, with bursting head, thought that it would never end.

"Tick, tock," proclaimed the old school clock, as the hands crept slowly to one, to two, to three.

"In five minutes I can go," thought poor little Anne wildly, and just then the school-room door opened, and on the threshold appeared a self-contained young lady in pale violet gingham, and the young lady was asking for Anne Batcheller!

"Judy!" said Anne's heart, with a bound, but her lips were still.

Miss Mary had seen the Judge's grand-daughter at church the day before, and had been much impressed, and now when Judy asked sweetly if Anne could go, she gave immediate consent.

"Of course she may," she said. "Anne, you are dismissed."

But her eyes did not meet Anne's eyes as she said it, for Miss Mary's head was better, and she was beginning to wonder if she should not have investigated before she condemned Anne so harshly.

Twenty-four heads turned towards the window as Anne and Judy climbed into the fascinating trap with the fawn cloth cushions, and twenty-four pairs of lungs breathed sighs of envy, as Judy picked up the reins, and the two little girls drove away together in the sunshine.

CHAPTER X

MISTRESS MARY

No one ever knew how Judy managed to get the Judge's consent, but on Wednesday, when the children on their way home from school called at the post-office for the mail, they found small square envelopes addressed to themselves, and each envelope contained a card, and on the card was written an invitation to every child to be present at a lawn party to be given at Judge Jameson's on the following Saturday, from one until five o'clock.

But this was not all. For during the evening, rumors, started by the wily Launcelot, leaked out, that never in the history of Fairfax had there been such a party as the one to be given by Judge Jameson in honor of his grand-daughter, Judith, and her friend, Anne Batcheller.

"For it is as much Anne's party as Judy's," Launcelot stated, as one having authority.

After the first jubilation, however, the young people looked at each other with blank faces.

"It is the same afternoon as the school entertainment," wailed Amelia Morrison.

"An' we've got to speak our pieces," said little Jimmie Jones.

But Nannie May cut the Gordian knot with her usual impetuosity.

"I am going to Judy's party," she declared, "and I am going to get mother to write a note to Miss Mary."

Many were the notes that went to Miss Mary that day. All sorts of excuses were given by the ambitious mothers, who would not have had their offspring miss the opportunity of seeing the inside of the most exclusive house in Fairfax for all the school entertainments in the world!

And Miss Mary!

She had invited the school board and a half-dozen pedagogues from neighboring districts. She had trained the children until they were letter perfect. She had drilled them in their physical exercises until they moved like machines, and now at the eleventh hour they were fluttering away from her like a flock of unruly birds, and she recognized at once that Judy had championed Anne's cause, and that in her she had an adversary to be feared.

In vain she expostulated with the mothers.

"Saturday isn't a regular school-day, you know, Miss Mary," said Mrs. Morrison, sitting down ponderously to argue the question with the teacher, "and of course the Judge couldn't know that it would interfere with your plans."

Miss Mary was convinced that the Judge *did* know, but she didn't quite dare to argue the question with him. She was conscious that she had been over-severe, and that the Judge, who believed in justice first, last, and all the time, would not uphold her.

And so the plans for the party went on.

"We will have games," said Judy, "and we won't have anything old like 'Cinderella.' Has anybody got an idea?"

She and Anne and Launcelot were in the Judge's garden, and it was Thursday evening, and there wasn't a great deal of time to get ready for Saturday's festivities.

"We might have some one read poems, and have living pictures to illustrate them," suggested Anne.

"What poems?" asked Judy, not quite sure that she liked the idea.

"There are some lovely things in Tennyson," said the little girl; "there's the Sleeping Beauty for one. You could be the Beauty, Judy, and Launcelot could be the prince - it would be just lovely - we could have little Jimmie Jones for the page, and Nannie and Amelia for ladies-in-waiting, and you could be asleep on the couch, while some one read:

"Year after year unto her feet,
She lying on her couch alone,
Across the purple coverlet,
The maiden's jet-black hair has grown."

Anne quoted with ease, for the little blue and gold volume in her bookcase had yielded up its treasures to her, and she knew the loved verses better than she knew her "Mother Goose."

"Oh," Judy's eyes were alight, "how lovely that is - I never read that, Anne."

"Well, you hate books, you know," and Anne dimpled at her retort.

"I shouldn't hate that kind," and Judy resolved that she would know more about that princess.

"And we could have the arrival of the prince, and the awakening, and their departure:

"And o'er the hills and far away,
Beyond their utmost purple rim,
Beyond the night, across the day,
Through all the world she followed him,"

chanted Anne like one inspired.

Then she blushed and blushed as the astonished Launcelot and Judy praised her.

"I never dreamed that you knew so much poetry," cried Launcelot, seeing her in a new and more respectful light.

"Oh, it just sings itself," said Anne. "When you read it a few times you can't help reciting it."

"But I am not going to be the only one," said Judy. "What part will you take, Anne?"

"I don't know."

"Who's your favorite heroine in Tennyson, Anne?" asked Launcelot.

"Elaine."

"Then Elaine it shall be -"

"And you must be Lancelot," cried Anne, eagerly.

"But he *is* Launcelot," said puzzled Judy.

Anne and Launcelot laughed. "Well, you see," said Anne, "in the poem Elaine is in love with a knight named Lancelot, and he doesn't love her, and she dies, and when she is dead they put her on a barge and send her to the court of King Arthur, where Lancelot is one of the knights, and there is a letter to him in her hand, and a lily, and it's lovely," she finished breathlessly.

"We shall have a hard time to build a barge," said Launcelot, with a shake of his head.

"But we must have that scene, Launcelot," insisted Anne.

"Never mind," said Judy, who believed that all difficulties could be surmounted in this line, "we will find something. How many pictures shall we have for 'Elaine,' Anne?"

"We could have her giving him the 'red sleeve broider'd with pearls,' and then we could have him ill in the cave, and the scene in the garden, and at her window when he rides away, and then on the barge."

"We'll have to outline the story," said Launcelot; "the poem would be too long."

"But we could get in some of it, like the little song about Love and Death," said Anne, anxiously, for being too young to know tragedy or love, she was yet enamoured by that which was beyond her comprehension.

It took all the next day for them to get things ready, but everything went beautifully. Dr. Grennel promised to read the poems. Perkins, though depressed at the prospect of more undignified gayety, gave permission to use the dining-room for the tableaux, and the little grandmother promised to spend all of Saturday with the Judge and his sister, thus giving Anne a crowning delight.

And then, at the last minute, Anne spoiled everything!

"I can't bear to think of poor Miss Mary," she sobbed, late on Saturday morning, when Judy found her crouched up in the window-seat overlooking the garden.

"What?"

"I can't bear to think about poor Miss Mary," repeated Anne, dabbing her eyes with her wet handkerchief.

"What's the matter?" asked Launcelot, as Judy stood speechless. He was outside of the window, where he was helping Perkins place the tables and arrange the chairs in the garden.

Anne's woebegone face bobbed up over the window-sill.

"I can't bear to think of Miss Mary. All alone while we shall be having such a good time," she wailed. "I wish we could invite her."

Judy stamped her foot. "Anne Batcheller," she cried, tempestuously, "you are too good to live," and she went out of the room like a whirlwind.

She went straight to the Judge and Mrs. Batcheller, who were chatting together in the dimness and quiet of the great parlor.

"I sha'n't have anything to do with the lawn party, grandfather," she blazed, after she had told her story, "if that teacher is to be invited!"

But the Judge's eyes were dreamy. "Dear little tender-heart," he said.

"She teaches us a lesson of forgiveness," said Mrs. Batcheller, who with the Judge had deeply resented the treatment accorded Anne on that fateful Monday morning.

"Perhaps it would be best to ask Miss Mary," ventured the Judge.

"If she would come," said Mrs. Batcheller, doubtfully.

But Judy would not listen to reason or argument.

"Do you think we ought to back down now," she demanded of Launcelot, who, with Anne, had followed her to the parlor to talk things over.

"No," he said, slowly, "I don't think we ought to back down. But I guess we shall have to."

"Why?"

Launcelot's eyes went to the sobbing figure in the little grandmother's arms.

"We can't make her unhappy," he said in a low voice.

"Anne?"

"Yes."

"Everything is spoiled now," said Judy, chokingly, "everything. And I took such an interest. I think it's mean - mean - mean -"

Her voice grew very shrill, and her face was red. Mrs. Batcheller started to speak, but the Judge raised his hand to stop the untimely lecture.

"Wait!" he said.

Something in his kind old face reminded Judy suddenly of the story he had told her just a week before - of her grandmother and how she had conquered her temper.

With a strong effort she kept back the words of furious disappointment that she had intended to hurl at these weak-spirited people. Then she whisked out of the room and down the hall, and presently Launcelot, who had followed her, came back laughing but mystified.

"She is walking around the oval in the garden," he said, "as fast as she can go, and she won't stop."

The Judge slapped his hand on his knee. "By George," he said, with a sigh of relief, "she's done it!" But when Anne asked him to explain, he shook his head. "That's a secret between Judy and me," he said, "and I can't tell it," and over her head he smiled at Mrs. Batcheller, who knew the story, and had often laughed with Judy's grandmother over it.

Judy came in, finally, rosy and breathless.

"Oh, invite your Miss Mary if you want to," she panted, as she kissed the tear-streaked face. "But don't expect me to act too saint-like. I am not made of the same stuff that you are, Anne."

"You are a brick," Launcelot pronounced later, when they were alone in the dining-room superintending the putting up of the stage; "it was harder for you to give up than for Anne."

"No, I'm not a brick." said Judy, a little wearily, "I am just hateful. But I do try," and his praise meant much to her, and helped her afterwards.

Miss Mary sat alone and discouraged when the note of invitation was handed to her. She had sent letters to the school board and the other teachers, pleading "unavoidable postponement," and now she was correcting papers with an aching head.

"Dear Miss Mary," - said Anne's little note, - "Please come to our party to-day. It is going to be very nice, and we are sorry we set the same day as the school entertainment, and we won't be happy if you are not here. Please forgive us, and come. Your affectionate scholar, Anne." And below the Judge had added, "I am anxious to supplement Anne's invitation and apology and to say with her, 'Please forgive us and come.'"

"I won't go," said Miss Mary at first, bitterly.

But when she had read the little letter again, she changed her mind.

"She is a dear child," she said.

And she washed her face and combed her hair, and put on her best white dress and her new summer hat with the roses in it, and went out looking young and pretty and with her headache forgotten.

And when she arrived at the Judge's she was escorted to a seat of honor in the front row, with the Judge on one side, and the little grandmother on the other, and with the astonished children smiling welcomes to her as she went up the aisle.

CHAPTER XI

THE PRINCESS AND THE LILY MAID

As the children arrived they were shown at once into the great dining-room, where at one end a stage had been erected and a curtain hung, from behind which came the sounds of hammering and subdued directions, given in Launcelot's voice.

"Amelia Morrison and Nannie May are in it," explained Tommy who had yearned for an important part, but Judy had declared against him.

"You shouldn't have been asked at all," she said, witheringly, "if it hadn't been that Anne begged that you might. You acted dreadfully the other day. Anne wouldn't have been punished if you had spoken right out, Tommy, and had said that it was your fault."

"Aw - yes, she would, too," stammered Tommy.

"I never could stand a coward," was Judy's fling, and at that Tommy subsided.

Behind the scenes Anne, in an entrancing trailing gown of pale blue with pearls wound in her long fair braids was trying to get Jimmie Jones to shut his eyes without opening his mouth.

"But I always sleep with my mouth open," persisted Jimmie, who, in spite of his yellow curls and his page's costume of green satire was at heart just plain boy.

"Well, you shouldn't," scolded Anne, as she tripped over her train. "You will simply spoil the picture. Just see how nice Judy and Amelia and Nannie look."

On the couch lay Judy all in soft, shining, satiny white, her dark hair spreading over the pillow, and one hand under her cheek; and at each end, Nannie and Amelia, in rose color and in violet, blissfully happy, and, though their eyes were closed, wide awake to the charms of the situation.

"Now - ready," whispered Anne, as Dr. Grennell's fine voice rolled out the last lines of the "Prologue." "Now -" and the curtain went up on "The Sleeping Princess."

Jimmie's mouth flew open and Amelia smiled, but little cared the gaping audience for such trifles. Breathless they stared as one scene followed another. Launcelot was a Prince that set all the little girls' hearts a-flutter, as he knelt beside the couch, with a great bunch of dewy roses in his arms, which, in the next picture, lay all scattered over Judy, when she waked and gazed at him dreamily. Jimmie came out strongly at this point, with a prodigious yawn that almost broke him in two, and was so expressive of great weariness that little Bobbie Green, his bosom friend, was carried away by the realism of it, and asked in awe, "Did he really sleep a hundred years?" and was not quite brought back to earth by Tommy Tolliver's exclamation, "Why you saw him awake this morning, Bobbie, didn't you?"

The Prince and the Princess went away together at last; she with a long velvet cloak covering the whiteness of her gown, and a hat with white plumes, and he with a sword at his side, that made Tommy Tolliver turn green with envy.

Jimmie Jones came down and sat by Bobbie Green during the intermission, in which lemonade was passed and the pictures discussed.

Bobbie gazed upon him as one who has come from a strange country.

"Say, say," he whispered eagerly, "how could you sleep when we was makin' all that noise, Jimmie - clappin'?"

Jimmie took a long blissful gulp of lemonade, and then fished out the strawberry from the bottom of the glass. "Ho," he said, "that wasn't nothin'. It wasn't really me that was asleep, it was just my eyes," and Bobbie, though still hazy, accepted the explanation and fished for his strawberry in imitation of his distinguished friend and actor, Jimmie Jones!

Most of the children had read parts of "Elaine" at school, and they "Oh-ed" and "Ah-ed" as the fair-haired heroine appeared.

Anne was very sweet, very appealing, as she went through the sad little scenes, and when at last she sat at the window. Dr. Grennell did not read Elaine's song, but Anne sang it, to Judy's accompaniment, played softly behind the scenes.

> "Sweet is true love, tho' given in vain, in vain;
> And sweet is death who puts an end to pain:
> I know not which is sweeter, no, not I."

And all the little girls wept into their handkerchiefs, while the boys sniffed audibly.

"Bless their hearts," said Mrs. Batcheller to Miss Mary, "it's too bad to have them cry."

But the Judge, who was a keen observer of human nature, shook his head. "A little sadness now and then won't hurt them," he said. "It is the shadows that make us appreciate the sunshine, you know."

There was a long wait before the curtain was raised on the last picture in the poem: "The dead steer'd by the dumb."

The barge had been a problem, until Judy solved it by placing an ironing-board across two chairs, and draping the whole into the semblance of a boat-like bier.

Perkins, under protest, was pressed into service as the dumb boatman, and with a long beard of white cotton, and a cloak and hood of funereal black, he was a picturesque and pessimistic figure.

"It's so wobbly," said Anne, powdered with corn-starch to an interesting paleness and draped all in white. "It's so wobbly, Judy," and she shrieked softly, as she laid herself flat on the ironing-board.

"Steady," advised Launcelot, as he shifted her carefully to the center, "now for the lily and the letter, Judy," and he threw over the prostrate Anne a yellow silk shawl of Judy's which was to serve as cloth of gold.

"Now, Perkins," and Perkins climbed to the high stool, which had been set in an armchair and formed the bow of the boat.

"If I falls, I falls," said Perkins, classically, "and my blood be on your head, sir," and while Judy writhed in agonies of laughter, Launcelot turned off the lights and adjusted the great lantern, which was to throw on the barge the effect of moonlight, while all else was to be in shadow.

The illusion from the front was perfect. Even the green piano cover with its dots of white cotton foamed up around the barge like real waves.

"How lovely she is," whispered all the children, as Anne lay there so still and quiet, with her fair hair streaming over the blackness of the bier.

"I don't like it. I don't like it," whimpered Bobbie Green, whose imagination was a thing to be reckoned with. "I don't like it. Anne, oh, Anne -"

And Anne's tender heart could not withstand that cry of fear.

"I'm all right, darling," she said, right out, and then the tension was broken, and all the children laughed, with relief, as Elaine sat up smiling and waving her hand to them.

"Bobbie Shafto" came next and was a dig at Tommy.

Judy's great marine picture made the background, and on the shore little Mary Morrison bade little Jimmie Jones "Good-bye" with heartrending sobs. But this Bobbie Shafto never went to sea. As picture followed picture, he was shown pulling at a rowing machine, sailing toy ships in a tub, fishing in a pail, and digging for treasure in a tiny sand pile - and after each funny scene, the curtain would drop, and tiny Mary Morrison would come to the front and wail:

> "*Tommy* Shafto's gone to sea,
> Silver buckles on his knee,
> He'll come back and marry me,
> Pretty *Tommy* Shafto!"

It brought down the house, but Tommy got very red and murmured in Bobbie's ear that "They might think it was funny, but *he* didn't," which Bobbie Green did not understand in the least.

"That's all," and Launcelot gave a sigh of relief, as Mary and Jimmie made their bows amid uproarious applause. He had been stage manager as well as actor, and he was tired.

"No, no," whispered Judy, as she came on the stage dressed as a fishermaid, and dragging a great net behind her. "No, no. Dr. Grennell is going to read 'Break, break, break.' I sha'n't need any change of scene. Just leave the big picture, and put this net and the shells around, and smooth out that sand to look like the beach."

She was making a rock out of two boxes covered with a gray

mackintosh as she spoke. "Now, if you could just whistle like the wind," she said. "Do you think you could, Launcelot?"

"I'll try," and he did whistle, so effectively, that he did not get his breath for five minutes.

Judy had read the poem one day when she was helping Anne to plan the pictures, and it had, like all songs of the sea, sung itself into her heart.

Again the big picture with its stretch of sea made the background, and Judy sat on the rock looking at it. The plaid lining of her mackintosh showed, and the wind sounded wheezy, but the pathos in Judy's face, the tragedy in her eyes as the third verse was read:

"And the stately ships go on,
To the haven under the hill,
But oh, for the touch of a vanished hand,
And the sound of a voice that is still!"

made the Judge wipe his eyes, and Mrs. Batcheller say hurriedly, "She should not have done it. She should not."

And behind the dropped curtain Judy was saying to Dr. Grennell, "I want to go back to the sea. I hate the country. I want to go back to the wind and waves. I can't stand it here."

But the doctor put his hand on her shoulder and looked down into her troubled face with grave eyes.

"Not now," he said, quietly, "not while your grandfather needs you, Judy."

Judy drew a long breath, then she put out her hand as if to make him a promise.

"No, not while grandfather needs me," she said, "not while he needs me, Doctor."

CHAPTER XII

LORDLY LAUNCELOT

The children of the town of Fairfax never forgot that afternoon at Judge Jameson's. For years they had peeped through the hedge at the fascinating Cupid of the Fountain, but never had one of them put foot in the old garden, with its mysterious nooks and formal paths, which lay in the shadow of the Great House.

But to-day with its gipsy band playing wild music, with its gaily decorated tables, its awe-inspiring Perkins, - who with his satellites offered food fit for the gods, - with its riot of spring color, it was beyond their wildest dreams.

Before they went home they all assembled again in the great dining-room from which the chairs had been taken, and on the polished floor every one, old and young, danced the Virginia Reel, the Judge leading with Miss Mary, and Mrs. Batcheller bringing up at the end of the line with Jimmie Jones.

"It was a success, wasn't it," said Launcelot, when the children had trooped away, and Anne and Mrs. Batcheller and the smiling Miss Mary had been driven home in the Judge's carriage.

"Yes," said Judy, abstractedly, watching the musicians, who were having their refreshments under the lilac bushes.

Temple Bailey

"What handsome faces they have," she said, "so dark and wild. And their lives are so free - grandfather says they just roam around from place to place, living in the woods and picking up a little money here and there. He says their camp is just outside, and when he was driving yesterday, he saw one of them playing and asked them if they wouldn't come here to-day."

When the gipsies had finished they rose and went down the path towards the gate. They were talking and laughing with a vivacious play of feature and a recklessness of gesture that proclaimed them the unconscious children of nature.

"How I wish I could go with them," said Judy, impulsively, as the young leader of the band took off his hat and waved them a debonair "good-bye." "How I wish I could go!"

But Launcelot shook his head. "It's all very romantic from the outside," he said, "but the women don't have a very good time. They tramp the dusty roads in summer and almost freeze in their open wagons in the winter, and they bear most of the burdens. Those men are handsome, all right, but some of them are brutes."

As he spoke the leader of the band came back up the path.

"Come to our camp, pretty lady," he said, flashing his dark eyes upon Judy, "and our queen will tell your fortune. For a piece of silver she will tell you the things that are past and the things that are to come."

"Oh, will she?" asked Judy, eagerly. "Will you be at the camp next Saturday?"

"We will be there until you come," said the gipsy with a glance of admiration at her vivid face.

But Launcelot's hand was clenched at his side. He did not like that fellow's face or his manner, he told himself, and Judy should not go near that camp if he could help it.

"You don't want to have your fortune told, Judy," he said, a little roughly.

Judy's eyebrows went up in surprise. "I do," she said. "It's fun."

"It's silly," contended Launcelot, doggedly.

The gipsy's eyes flashed from one to the other.

"You will come," he urged, ignoring Launcelot, and addressing his question to Judy.

"Yes."

"On Saturday?"

"Yes."

"Good; we will welcome you, pretty lady." And with a defiant glance at the big angry boy, the dark Hungarian swung down the path, singing as he went.

"You are not going," said Launcelot, when the man was out of sight.

"I am."

"Then I shall tell the Judge."

"Telltale."

Launcelot stood up and glowered at her.

"Who do you think will go with you?"

"You." There was a laugh in Judy's eyes, as she made the

impertinent answer.

"I won't."

"Not if I ask you?"

"Not under any circumstances. It isn't the place for you, Judy."

Then he sat down beside her. "Look here," he said, in a wheedling tone, "if I were really your big brother, I wouldn't let you go. Can't you let me order you around a little, just as if I were -?"

Judy caught her breath. Why would he use that tone? It always made her feel as if she wanted to give in - but she wouldn't.

"I am going," she said, slowly, although she did not look at him, "if I have to go alone."

"Then I shall tell the Judge."

"Oh," Judy's tone was cutting, "I always did hate boys."

For a moment Launcelot's face flamed, then most unexpectedly he laughed.

"You don't hate me, Judy," he said, "you know you don't."

"I do."

"No, you don't," he went on, and there was no anger in his voice, only good-natured tolerance that made Judy's temper seem very childish. "You are angry now. But you are not that kind of girl -"

"What kind of girl?"

"Changeable."

"Oh, I don't know."

But Launcelot insisted. "You are not changeable, Judy, and you know it."

And finally Judy gave in. "No, I'm not, and I don't hate you, but I hate to be told I can't do things."

"You will have to get used to it - " daringly.

"Oh - you needn't think *you* can order me around, Launcelot, in that lordly way -"

She faced him defiantly. Her eyes were glowing with excited feeling. She looked like a young duchess in her anger. After the pictures, she had twisted her hair on top of her head in shining coils, and the dress she wore was a quaint mull that had been her grandmother's, a thing of creamy folds and laces that swept the floor. Launcelot felt suddenly very crude and impertinent to be dictating to this very stately young lady. But her next remark made her a child again, and brought him confidence.

"I have always had my own way - and I shall do as I please."

Launcelot got up lazily. "All right," he said, and held out his hand, "good-bye. I promised mother that I wouldn't be late."

But Judy did not seem to see the hand. She leaned against one of the big pillars indifferently, and looked out over the garden, Launcelot waited a moment, and then his hand dropped.

"Oh, I suppose you and I will have to quarrel now and then," he said, "we are both so obstinate," and he smiled to himself as Judy frowned darkly at the word, "but I don't see any use in doing it now, when we have had such a nice day -"

With one of her quick changes of mood Judy beamed on him. "Oh, hasn't it been nice," she said. And then she held out her hand. "Good-bye," she smiled.

But as he went down the path she called after him.

"If you meet Tommy Tolliver, tell him I want to see him."

He stopped. "What do you want him for?" he asked, suddenly suspicious.

"I sha'n't tell you."

"You needn't think you can get him to take you to the gipsy camp," said Launcelot.

"He will take me if I ask him."

"No, he won't."

"Why not?"

"Because I shall tell him beforehand that if he takes you out there I shall thrash him within an inch of his life."

"What?" gasped Judy.

"I shall do it," said Launcelot, and as he swung down the path, Judy, looking after the straight, strong figure, knew that his threat was not an idle one.

And yet, after all, if it had not been for Launcelot, Judy would never have gone to the camp. She had debated the question and had decided that the game was not worth the candle. She had approached Tommy Tolliver, and his numerous excuses convinced her that Launcelot had been before her. She had hinted her wishes to Anne, only to be met by that virtuous maiden with "Oh, Judy, I should be afraid - they look so dark and wild - and besides we ought not to go -" She even suggested a drive to the camp to the Judge, but he had said: "It is not a place for you, my dear," as if that settled the question.

Then, too, she had other plans for Saturday, for Launcelot

planned to drive his mother and Judy and Anne to Lake Limpid, and they were to take an early boat for a little resort where they were to meet some of Mrs. Bart's friends.

Judy stayed with Anne all night, so as to be as near the Barts as possible, for there was a drive of five miles, and the boat left at eight o'clock.

"Do get up, Judy," begged Anne, on Saturday morning, as she stood in front of her little mirror, her hair combed, her shoes polished, and her last bow tied.

But Judy dug her rumpled head deeper into the pillow.

"'If you're waking, call me early, call me early, mother, dear,'" she murmured, having improved her acquaintance with Tennyson during the week.

"Well, it isn't early," said Anne, sharply. "You will be late, Judy, and we must catch the boat."

Judy sat up rubbing her eyes. "Oh, it won't hurt Launcelot to wait a little. He thinks he can manage everybody - but he can't dictate to me, Anne. I am not as meek as you are."

"I'm not meek," flared Anne, whose usually sweet temper had been somewhat ruffled in her efforts to wake Judy. "But Launcelot is a very sensible boy."

"Oh, sensible," groaned Judy. "I *hate* sensible people."

"What kind of people do you like?" demanded Anne, indignantly. "Unsensible ones?"

"Yes. Dashing people and lively people and funny people - and - and - romantic people - but sensible people, oh, dear," and she buried her head again in the pillow.

"Judy, *get up*."

"I'll be ready in time."

"No, you won't. And breakfast is ready. Judy, get up."

A gentle snore was the only answer.

"Oh," and Anne flung herself out of the room, "if you are late, Judy Jameson, I can't help it."

She went down-stairs and ate her breakfast. But no sign of Judy.

"Judee - ee!" she called up the stairway, and "Judee - ee!" she called again from the garden, where, with Belinda and Becky, she stood awaiting the arrival of the carriage.

"Judith, my dear," expostulated the little grandmother, climbing the stairway slowly, "Judith, my dear, you really must hurry. You will have to go without any breakfast - I -"

She opened the door of the little bedroom and stopped short.

The bedclothes had been thrown over the foot-board, the pillows were on the floor, Judy's clothes were gone, and the room was empty!

CHAPTER XIII

A FORTUNE AND A FRIGHT

"She is hiding," said Anne.

But though they hunted and called, not a sign of the missing girl could they find.

When Launcelot came, Anne was almost in tears.

"She must be here somewhere," she said. "It's too bad. We shall be late."

"No, we won't," said Launcelot, who had listened without a word to the tale of Judy's shortcomings and final disappearance. "We will not be late, Anne, for if Judy doesn't come in just three minutes, we will go without her."

"Oh, no, no, no," protested Anne, all her grievances against Judy forgotten in the face of such a calamity. "We can't leave her behind."

"She will leave herself behind," said Launcelot, "for mother can't miss the boat. She has promised her friends that she will meet them."

"But my dear," protested gentle Mrs. Bart, "we can surely wait until the last minute. Judy only intends it as a joke, and it is too bad to leave her."

Temple Bailey

But Launcelot was in an explosive mood. The morning had been a trying one for him. He had hurried through a half-day's work in an hour and a half, he had eaten hardly any breakfast for fear he should keep the girls waiting, and now - to be treated like this!

"We can't wait any longer," he said, looking at his watch. "I am sorry, Anne, but we shall just have to leave Judy behind."

Again Anne started to protest, but the little grandmother shook her head. "Judy deserves it," she said. "She is too old to be so childish."

"Maybe she is waiting down the road somewhere," said Anne, hopefully. "I think she is trying to fool us."

But Judy was not waiting down the road. She was in the orchard behind the plum-tree.

"It won't hurt Launcelot to wait," she had, thought as she hid herself, "I will make him think I am not going -"

But she had not dreamed that they would go without her, and when she saw Anne climb in and the carriage start off, she ran forward wildly.

"Wait," she called, "wait for me."

But the carriage whirled on in a cloud of dust, and her voice echoed on the empty air.

By the time Judy reached the house Mrs. Batcheller had gone in, and so the little girl ran down the road unseen. "Perhaps they will stop for me," she thought, and her eyes were strained after the flying vehicle.

But it did not stop, and at last warm and tired Judy dropped down by the roadside, a forlorn figure.

"I didn't think they would leave me," she thought disconsolately.

After a while she got up and started towards the house. She dreaded to face Mrs. Batcheller, however, and she sat down again to decide upon a plan for spending the day.

She would not stay in the little gray cottage, that was a sure thing, and to go back to the Judge's meant a dull day by herself.

As she mused, a cheery whistle sounded down the road. "A Life on the Ocean Wave" was the tune and Judy started to her feet.

"Oh, Tommy Tolliver, Tommy Tolliver," she called, "come here."

Tommy rounded the curve in the road and stared at her.

"Say, I thought you were going with Anne," he said. "They just passed me down the road."

"Did they?" asked Judy, indifferently. "Well, at the last minute I thought I wouldn't go."

"Well, you missed it," said Tommy, aggravatingly. "Lake Limpid's great - and Launcelot can sail a boat like anything."

"Oh, can he?" said Judy, faintly. She loved to sail, and Tommy's words brought before her a vision of the pleasure she had forfeited.

There was silence for several minutes, then Judy said:

"Tommy, do you know where the gipsies are camping?"

Tommy waved her away.

"I can't take you there," he said, "I have promised I won't."

"'Nobody asked you, sir, she said,'" Judy's tone was withering. "I asked you where it was."

"Oh."

"Well, tell me."

Tommy wriggled.

"Are you going there?"

"Perhaps."

"Well, you'd better not. Launcelot won't like it."

"Oh, Launcelot, Launcelot." Judy's voice was scornful. "I don't care what Launcelot likes, Tommy Tolliver."

"Oh, don't you?" cried Tommy, brightening. "Well, then -"

But he stopped suddenly. "No, I can't tell you," he said, miserably.

"Why not?"

"I can't.

"Oh, well, you needn't," said Judy. "But I can find out. And I'm going."

"You'd better not," warned Tommy, yet hoping she would do it.

"I'll go with you," he agreed, "if you will promise not to tell."

"I don't want you to go," asserted Judy. "I want you to tell me how to get there."

Tommy told her as well as he could.

"That doesn't seem very clear," said Judy, when he had finished. "But I guess I can find it - and Tommy" - she fixed him with a stern glance - "don't you tell any one where I am - not any one - or I sha'n't ever speak to you again -"

"All right," said Tommy. "And don't you let on to Launcelot that I told you which way to go."

"Good-bye," said Judy.

"Good-bye," said Tommy.

And off they started in different directions, feeling like a pair of conspirators.

For the first half-mile Judy enjoyed her walk. The sky was blue, and the air was soft, and there were violets on the banks and forget-me-nots in the field, and the orchards were pink with bloom.

There were birds everywhere, from the great black crows, strutting over the red hills of newly planted corn, to the tiny gray sparrows, that slipped through the dusty grass at the roadside.

And in spite of the fact that she had started on a forbidden quest, Judy was happy. For the first time since she had come to the Judge's she was alone and free - with no reckoning to come until evening.

She stepped along lightly, but after a while she went more slowly, and by the time she reached the thick piece of woodland where the gipsies were encamped, she was tired out. They were not far from the road, for she could hear the thrum of the guitars, and voices raised as if in a quarrel.

The voices were stilled as Judy's white-gowned figure appeared under the over-arching oaks.

The dark young leader, who had been at the Judge's, uttered something in a warning voice to a sullen young woman who lounged against a pile of bright-colored rugs, and with whom he had been having evidently a fierce argument. She wore a soiled, silken cap, loaded with gilt coins, and her dress was in tawdry reds and yellows, yet picturesque and becoming to her dark beauty. She stared insolently at Judy as the latter came forward, but the young leader was smiling and profuse in his welcome.

"You have come," he said, "and alone?"

Something in his tone made Judy draw away from him.

"Yes," she said, and then, peremptorily, "I want my fortune told."

"I will speak to the queen," he said, and left her, with another of his flashing smiles.

The camp life as Judy looked upon it presented an alluring picture to one of her romantic turn of mind. Back in the darkness and dimness of a cave-like opening in the rocks, an old woman bent over a charcoal brazier. Her hair, gray and grizzled, fell over a yellow face that, lighted by the blue flames, took on a hag-like aspect. Her skinny hands moved as if in incantations, and Judy shivered with the mystery of it until the strong and unmistakable odor of beef and onion stew rose on the air and relieved her mind as to the nature of the brew which might have been of "wool of bat and tongue of dog" for all she knew to the contrary.

A group of swarthy men lounged under the trees and down by the stream a half-dozen children played with a half-dozen dogs. The children were fat and rosy, and the curs lean and cadaverous, and the dozen of them had stared at Judy as she came into the camp in animal-like curiosity, and then had gone on with their playing.

From one of the two big wagons drawn up near the road came the wailing of an infant, and in the other a woman, half-hidden by the curtain, sat weaving a bright-colored basket.

"Do you all work at basket weaving?" Judy asked the silent girl on the rugs.

"I do not work," was the answer. Then she tossed her head, defiantly. "I will not work. They cannot make me."

She started to say more, but she stopped as the dark young leader came back.

He had spoken to the old woman who presided at the fire, and Judy saw her wipe her hands and make for a dilapidated tent under an oak.

It was to this tent that she was directed, and when she was once within and her eyes had grown accustomed to the darkness, she saw the old hag, looking more witch-like than ever, with her head tied up in a flaming yellow bandanna, and her shoulders wrapped in a great cloak covered with cabalistic signs.

"Cross my hand with silver," she murmured, and Judy took out the only piece of money she had with her - a silver quarter of a dollar.

The old woman looked at it with dissatisfaction. "That is not enough," she said. "I can tell you nothing for that."

"But I haven't any more," said Judy, in dismay. "I didn't expect to come, and it is all I have."

"Oh, well," grudgingly, "I will tell you a little."

She took Judy's hand in hers and studied the palm.

"You will live to be old," she said, monotonously. "There are double rings around your wrist. You will marry a man with wealth and with gray eyes."

"I don't want to know that -" said Judy, impatiently, to whom such matters were as yet unimportant. "Tell me about - about - other things."

"Hush," said the gipsy, "I must say, what I must say. You will go on a long journey. It will be on the sea. You will look for one who is lost. You are a child of the sea -" She flung Judy's hand away from her. "That is all," she said, heavily, "I can tell you no more without more money."

"Oh, oh," cried Judy, breathlessly, "how did you know it. How did you know that I was a child of the sea -"

"What I tell, I know," crooned the old woman, theatrically. "I can tell nothing without silver."

"But I haven't any more money," cried poor Judy.

"But a ring, a pin, they will do as well,"' the old woman looked at her greedily.

"I don't wear jewelry," said Judy, "I don't care for it."

"A chain, a charm, then," urged the old woman, whose eagle eyes had caught the outline of something that glittered beneath the thin lace collar of Judy's gown.

"I have nothing."

"There, there, - what have you there?" and the yellow finger tapped Judy's throat.

Judy drew back with a little shudder, and shook her head as she showed the thin gold chain with a pearl clasp on the end of which was a quaint silver coin.

"I couldn't let you have this," she said. "My mother always wore it. It is a Spanish coin. My father found two of them on the beach near our home, and he gave mother one, and he kept the other - they are just alike. Oh, no, I couldn't give you that -"

"I will tell you many things - about one who has gone away," tempted the old woman.

For a moment Judy wavered. "Oh, I can't," she decided. "I can't let you have this."

The old woman got up. "Then go," she said roughly.

All at once there came over Judy a feeling of fear. She turned quickly and saw the young leader in the door behind her. There was something sinister in his looks, and between the two she felt trapped.

"Let me out," she panted. "Let me out."

With a smile, the man in the door drew aside, and she stepped out into the daylight. As she did so, he whispered to the old woman, "What did you get?"

"Nothing. But the girl has on a chain with a pearl in it that would buy us food for a year."

"Oh!"

He followed Judy quickly.

"Stay, and we will play for you," he urged.

But her nerves were shaken.

"No, no," she said, hurriedly, "I must go home."

"You must stay until we play," he insisted, and called the men together, and Judy, still trembling from the moment of dread in the dark tent, sank down once more beside the sullen girl on the rugs.

But the leader called the girl away for a moment, and when she came back she sat closer to Judy than before, and her hand was busy with the fastening of the chain at the back - but so lightly, so deftly, that Judy sat unconscious.

And in the intervals of the music the girl laughed and chatted, telling Judy of the life on the road, of anything to hold her attention.

"You would look like one of us," she said, "if you wore one of these," and she threw across Judy's shoulders a scarf of red silk.

"I believe I am half gipsy," said Judy, trying to be agreeable, but shrinking with a feeling of repulsion from the untidy creature so near her.

The girl drew away the scarf with a loud laugh and a triumphant nod and a wink to the leader, and presently the music stopped.

"I must go," said Judy, more and more in dread of these strange people.

Once more the old woman bent over the blue flames; but the children had gone deeper into the wood, and the place was silent except for the occasional guttural remark of one of the men, or a wail from the baby in the wagon.

"I must go," she said again, and started off.

But when she reached the road, the young leader caught up with her.

"You are beautiful," he said, when he was beyond the hearing of the others.

Judy hurried on in silence, but he kept by her side. "You are beautiful," he said again, and laid his hand on her arm.

Then Judy whirled around on him. "Don't speak to me that way again," she said, imperiously. "I may be alone and helpless, and I know now that I was very foolish to come. But my grandfather is a Judge. If anything happens to me, he will call you to account. Go back to the camp. Go back and let me alone."

The man stopped short and gazed at her.

"You are brave," he said, in a more respectful tone.

"None of my family have ever been cowards," said Judy, who was herself again. "I am not afraid of you."

His bold eyes dropped before the fearlessness in hers.

"Good-bye," he said, humbly, and when he reached the edge of the camp he turned and looked after her, and there was a shadow on his swarthy face.

The girl on the pile of rugs called him.

"I got it," she said.

"Give it to me," he ordered, roughly. But she held the necklace away from him with a teasing laugh. "It is mine, it is mine," she cried, then shrieked, as he wrenched it out of her hand, twisting her wrist cruelly.

Judy, alone once more and with her courage all gone, so that she was so weak that she could hardly stand, ran on and on, blindly. She dared not go back the way she had come for fear of meeting again some of the hated band.

"I will keep ahead," she thought. "There must be a house somewhere, and I can get them to drive me home."

But though she walked on and on, no house appeared. She was faint with fatigue and hunger, and at last, as she came to the end of a road and found herself stranded in a great pasture, a sob caught in her throat.

She sat down on a rock and looked around. There seemed to be nothing in sight but rocks and scrubby bushes, and already twilight was descending over the land.

"I believe I am lost," she owned at last, "and if some one doesn't find me pretty soon, I shall have to stay out all night."

CHAPTER XIV

A PRECIOUS PUSSY CAT

The moon was out and the stars when Judy discovered a flock of sheep in the middle of the great pasture.

They were gathered together in a close woolly bunch as she came upon them, and they turned to her their mild white faces, but did not get up from the ground. It was nice to be near something alive, even if it was only such meek, silly creatures, and Judy sat down on a stone near them.

"I will stay here," she decided. "I simply cannot walk another step."

It was very lonely and she was very frightened. The moon lighted the world with a white light, but the shadows were black under the trees; somewhere in the distance a whippoorwill uttered a plaintive note, and from the gloomy woods beyond came the mournful hoot of an owl.

Judy slipped down to the softer grass, and resting her head on her arm gazed up at the sky, and gradually her fear went from her in the silence of the perfect night. A line marked in one of her father's books came to her:

"God's in his heaven
All's right with the world."

Judy did not know that Browning had said that - she didn't care who had said it, but it comforted her. If everything had seemed to go wrong in her own little world, it was because she had made it wrong. Here under the wonderful sky was peace, and if she was afraid and out of harmony it was her own fault.

"If I hadn't gone where I ought not to have been, nothing would have happened," was her rather mixed, if perfectly correct, summing up.

The little lambs bleated now and then:

"Maa-a-a, Maa-aa-a."

And the old ewes responded comfortingly,

"Baa-aa -" which Judy interpreted as meaning, "I am here, little one, don't be afraid."

"I won't be afraid either, you dear old thing," said Judy to the motherly creature near her, who had turned upon her now and then inquiring gentle eyes. "I won't be afraid, and I am going to sleep."

She did go to sleep, and when she waked, the world was dark. The moon had sailed away like a golden boat, and the stars seemed very far off.

Judy sat up and shivered. A cool wind had risen, but that was not what had roused her.

She had heard something!

Something that just at the right of the flock of sheep moved silently, something blacker than the darkness that enveloped it!

She thought of wild animals, of tramps, of everything natural that might invade a pasture; then as a sepulchral cry broke once more upon the air, she remembered all the tales she had ever heard of Things that visited one in the night.

"Judy Jameson, you know you don't believe in ghosts," she tried to reassure herself, "you know you don't, Judy Jameson," but all the same her heart went "thumpety-thump."

She cowered back against the rock as a white figure appeared beside the black one, and the two bore down upon her.

There was a sudden bewildering chorus:

"Caw - caw - caw -"

"Purr - rr - meow -"

And then Judy screamed, joyfully, "Oh, Belinda, Belinda, you precious pussy cat," and in her relief she hugged the great white animal, as if she were not the same girl who, not many days before, had said, "I hate cats."

Becky walked around in a circle and inspected Judy.

"So it was you, Becky, was it?" asked Judy, "that I saw first? But what made you look so tall?"

She went to the place where she had first seen the apparition, and found the slender stump of a tree, on top of which Becky had been perched.

"What are you doing here, so far from home, Belinda," asked Judy, as she sat down and took the purring, gentle creature in her lap.

But Belinda could not talk, although she patted Judy's hand with her paw and curled down with her head in the crook of Judy's arm.

"My, it's good to have you here," said Judy, "but I wonder how it happened."

She gathered the big cat close to her, grateful for the warmth of the soft body, and with Becky perched up on a rock behind, she sat very still, comforted by the sound of Belinda's sleepy song, and by Becky's sentinel-like watchfulness.

It was in the black darkness that precedes the dawn that she was roused by a lantern flashing across her eyes.

"Grandfather," she said, sleepily, as a haggard old face bent above her. "Grandfather."

"Judy," he said, with a break in his voice.

Wide-awake now, she saw that his hands trembled so that he had to set the lantern down.

"Oh," she said, remorsefully, as she sat up, "how tired you look, grandfather."

"We have hunted for you all night," he said, and the dim rays from the lantern showed the droop of his figure and the lines in his face.

"Oh, grandfather," she said again, and clung to him, sobbing softly.

"Hush," he said, holding her close. "Hush, Judy. You are all right now."

"Oh, I am all right," she sobbed, despairingly, "but it is you, grandfather, you are all tired out, and just because I was such - such - a silly goose -"

"Never mind, never mind," said the Judge, hastily, "I have found you now."

"I am not worth finding," said Judy, miserably, "I am not, grandfather."

But the Judge laughed at that, and smoothed her hair away from her forehead with a loving touch. "You are always my dear little girl," he assured her, "whatever you do - you know that, don't you?"

"Yes," she whispered, and laid her face against his sleeve.

"Now we will go back," he said presently, and with Belinda and Becky in close attendance, they went up the hill together.

At the top Judy gave a cry of astonishment, for right in front of her, on the other side of the hill, was the little gray house, ablaze with light.

"And I have been right back of it all night. If I had just walked a few steps farther," exclaimed Judy. "I must have gone in a circle, and I thought I was miles from here -"

As they came to the door the little grandmother met them, and Anne, and in the background Tommy Tolliver.

"We didn't know you were lost," explained Anne as she received the returned wanderer in her arms, "until we got back from Lake Limpid. Grandmother thought you had joined us down the road, and we thought you had stayed at home, and the Judge, of course, thought you were with me, and so none of us worried until we came back to-night and found you had been gone all day."

"And then Tommy told us that you had gone to the gipsy camp," went on Anne.

At Judy's reproachful glance Tommy burst out:

"I couldn't help telling, Judy. Launcelot made me."

"I should say I did," said a voice from the doorway, and Launcelot came in with Dr. Grennell. "I was sure he knew something about it."

Judy greeted them from the big rocking chair - where she sat big-eyed and weary, but a most interesting spectacle.

"Launcelot went to the camp and found that the gipsies had gone, so we knew you couldn't have seen them -" began the Judge, and at that Judy interrupted him.

"But I *did* see them, grandfather," she said, "I went to the camp."

"And were they there?" asked Launcelot

"Yes."

"Were they packing while you were there?"

"No."

"I wonder what made them leave so suddenly," and Launcelot and the Judge and Dr. Grennell looked at each other.

"Did you give them anything, Judy?" asked the Judge.

"Nothing but twenty-five cents. They were horrid, and the old woman wanted me to give my chain and Spanish coin. She knew an awful lot and I was crazy to hear the rest of my fortune, but I couldn't give away my coin."

"What coin, Judy?" asked Tommy, curiously.

"This one -" Judy put her hand to her neck, then she screamed:

"It's gone, grandfather. Launcelot, it's gone."

"What?" They all bent forward in excitement.

"I thought so," said the Judge, settling back in his chair, "when she said she had seen them, and then they disappeared before we could get to them. I thought they had been up to something."

"It was my chain with the pearl in it," said Judy, "the one you gave mother."

"Yes, and the rascals knew that the pearl was worth more than their whole outfit."

Launcelot picked up his hat. "I'm going to get it for you," he said, "they can't play any tricks like that."

"I'll go with you," said Dr. Grennell, "you may need an older man to help you. I think we can catch them with good horses."

He bent over Judy before he went out. "I wish you had come to me to have your fortune told," he said, "I could have told you more than that old hag."

"How?" asked Judy, puzzled.

"I should have told you that life is what we make it. And your fortune will be good or bad as you live it. It will not be a gipsy queen but Judy Jameson who shall decide the final issue."

"But, doctor, she knew that I loved the sea, and - and - that I had lost some one that I loved -"

"Oh, Judy," Launcelot's tone was impatient, "didn't you tell that fellow that you were coming, and didn't they have lots of time to find out about you."

"I didn't think of that." said Judy meekly.

But as he went out of the door, she had a little flash of temper.

"If you had waited for me this morning, I shouldn't have gone to the camp."

"If you had been ready, I shouldn't have left you," was Launcelot's reply, as his quiet eyes met Judy's stormy ones.

"Oh," she said, helplessly, and turned her gaze away, feeling that, as usual, he had the best of it.

And at that he whispered, "But I didn't have a good time, Judy - we - we missed - you -" and he followed Dr. Grennell.

"And now," said the little grandmother, "every one go home, and let me put this naughty girl to bed," but she smiled at Judy as she said it, and the tired little maid put her arms around her, and buried her face in the motherly bosom, and shook in a sudden chill.

"I am afraid she is going to be ill," said the Judge, anxiously, but the little grandmother tried to cheer him.

"She will be all right when she is rested," she said, with a confidence she did not really feel.

But when Anne was fast asleep, and Judy lay awake, tossing restlessly in the gray light of the dawn, the little grandmother came in, in a flannel wrapper, with her curls tucked away under a hand-made lace nightcap.

"Can't you sleep, dearie?" she whispered, as she sat down beside the bed.

"No. I think, and think, and think - about grandfather, and what a worry I am -" and Judy gave a great sigh.

"He has so many cares." The little grandmother's tone was gentle but it carried reproof, and Judy sat up and looked at her with troubled eyes.

"But I can't help my nature," she cried, tempestuously. "I can't bear to do things like other people, and when I get restless it seems as if I must go, and when I am angry I just have to say things -"

But the little grandmother shook her head. "You don't have to be anything you don't want to be, Judy," she said.

"But it seems so easy for Anne to be good," pursued Judy, "and so hard to me."

"It isn't always easy for Anne," said the little grandmother.

"Isn't it?" with astonishment.

"No, indeed. Anne has fought out many little fights of temper and wilfulness right here in this little room - she is a dear child."

"Indeed she is," agreed Judy, glancing at the serene face on the pillow.

"But Anne has learned to think for others. That is the secret, dearie. Think of your grandfather, think of your friends, and it will be wonderful how little time you will have to think of Judy Jameson."

"If I had my mother." Judy's lip quivered.

The little grandmother laid her old cheek against the flushed one.

"Dear heart," she said, "I can't take her place, but if you will try to talk to me as Anne does, maybe I can help -"

"I will," said Judy, and kissed her; but when the little grandmother had gone away, Judy could not sleep, and finally she got up and put on her red dressing-gown and sat by the window and looked out upon the waking world.

The robins were up and out on the dewy lawn, safe for once from Belinda, who was curled up sound asleep on the foot of

Anne's bed. Becky with her head under her wing was on top of the little bookcase, and the house was very quiet.

Suddenly through the mists of the morning Judy saw a carriage coming down the road.

It stopped at the gate and Launcelot leaped out.

Judy spoke to him from the window. "Hush," she said, "every one is asleep. I will come down."

As she met him at the lower door, he swung something bright and shining in front of her eyes.

"We found it," he whispered, excitedly, as Judy took her chain with a cry of delight. "We came across the gipsies on the Upper Fairfax road. The man tried to bluff it out, but the girl gave him away. While he was talking to Dr. Grennell she told me that he had it. I think she was mad at him about something, but she said he would kill her if he knew she told. So I just went on about the Judge and how he intended to put the police on the case if we didn't bring back the chain, and that he would be willing to hush it up if we got it, and so he handed it out - said it had been found on the ground after you left."

"Where is Dr. Grennell?" asked Judy.

"I dropped him at the manse," said Launcelot, "but I couldn't wait to bring this to you. I thought you would want to know about it."

"I couldn't sleep," explained Judy, "I was so afraid I had lost it."

"It's a funny coin, isn't it," said Launcelot. "Dr. Grennell knows a lot about such things, and he says it is a very old one."

"Yes," she told him. "Father found two of them on the beach

in front of our house, 'The Breakers.' There have been others found on the Maryland coast near it, and they say that a Spanish vessel was shipwrecked off there years ago, and that now and then some of the money washes in. The fishermen along the shore dig holes in the sand, and occasionally they find one of these."

"Well, you had better leave it at home the next time you go on a wild goose chase."

"There won't be any next time," said Judy, with a sober face.

Launcelot looked up from the coin with a quick smile, which faded as she gave a hoarse little cough.

"Go into the house, child," he ordered, "you will take cold out here -"

"Oh," in that moment Judy was herself again, tempestuous, defiant, "don't be so bossy, Launcelot."

"Go in," he said again, but she threw up her head and lingered.

"What a beautiful morning it is," she said. "Look, Launcelot, the sun, it is like a ball of gold through the mist."

But Launcelot was looking at her - at the melancholy little figure in the trailing red gown, with the dark hair braided down on each side of the white face, and hanging in a long braid at the back.

"Go in," he said, for the third time, peremptorily. "You are tired to death, and you will be sick -"

CHAPTER XV

THE SPANISH COINS

Three weeks after Judy's exciting experience at the gipsy camp, an interesting party of travellers were gathered on the platform at Fairfax station.

There was a stately old man, imposing in spite of a tweed cap and sack coat. By his side stood a slender girl in gray, who coughed now and then, and near them, perched on a brand-new trunk, which bore the initials "A. B." was a small maiden, resplendent in a modish blue serge, a scarlet reefer, a stiff sailor hat of unquestionable up-to-dateness, and tan shoes!

And the resplendent maiden was Anne!

"You must let her go to the seashore with us," the Judge had said to Mrs. Batcheller. "Judy hasn't been well since she took that heavy cold the night she stayed out in the pasture - and I know the child pines for the sea, although she doesn't say a word. And I don't want her separated from Anne. She needs young company."

The little grandmother consented reluctantly. She was very proud, and although for years the Judge had tried to do something substantial to help his old friend in her poverty, he had so far been unsuccessful in breaking down the barrier of independence which she had set up.

One promise he had wrung from her, however, that when Anne was old enough, he was to send her away to school, where she would be fitted to take her place worthily in a long line of cultured people. This he had demanded and obtained by virtue of his friendship for her father and grandfather, and for the "sake of Auld Lang Syne."

"But Anne's things will do very well," said Mrs. Batcheller, when the Judge tried tactfully to suggest that he be allowed to send Anne's order with Judy's.

"No, they won't," the Judge had insisted, bluntly, "Judy's old home at The Breakers is somewhat isolated, but there will be trips that the girls will take together, and friends will call, and I can't have little Anne unhappy because she hasn't a pretty gown to wear."

"Oh, well," sighed Mrs. Batcheller, "if you look at it that way. Now in my day, if a girl had a sweet temper and nice manners, that was all that was necessary."

"Hum -" mused the Judge. "But I remember somebody in a little white gown with green sprigs, and a hat with pink roses under the brim."

"Judith and I had them just alike," smiled the blushing little grandmother.

"And you looked like two sweet old-fashioned roses," said the old man, "and you knew it, too. The world hasn't changed so very much, or girl nature."

"Perhaps not," confessed the little grandmother, her eyes still bright with the memories of youthful vanities; "perhaps not, and you may have your way, Judge, only you mustn't spoil my little girl."

"She can't be spoiled," said the Judge promptly, and went away triumphant.

And so it came about that in the trunk on which Anne sat were five frocks - two white linen ones like Judy's; a soft gray for cool days, an organdie all strewn with little pink roses, and an enchanting pale blue mull for parties.

No wonder that Anne sat on that trunk!

It was a treasure casket of her dreams - and with the knowledge of what it contained, she did not envy Cinderella her godmother, nor Aladdin his lamp!

"Amelia and Nannie are coming to say 'good-bye,'" said Anne, as two figures appeared far up the road, "they'd better hurry."

"Tommy is coming, too," said Judy. "I wish I could take them all with me."

"Why not invite them all down to The Breakers," suggested the Judge, who was eager to do anything for this fragile, big-eyed granddaughter, who was creeping into his heart by gentle ways and loving consideration, so that he sometimes wondered if the old, tempestuous Judy were gone for ever.

"Not now," said Judy, thoughtfully. "I just want you and Anne for a while, but I should love to have them some time - and Launcelot, too."

"Can you?" she asked Launcelot, as he came out of the baggage room with their checks in his hand, followed by Perkins with the bags.

"Can I what?" he asked, standing before her with his hat in his hand, a shabby figure in shabby corduroy, but a gentleman from the crown of his well-brushed head to the soles of his shining boots.

"Will you come down to The Breakers sometime? - I am going to ask Amelia and Nannie and Tommy, and I want you, too -"

"Will I come? Well, I should say I would - " but suddenly his smile faded. "I am awfully afraid I can't, though. There is so much to do around our place, and father isn't well."

Now in spite of the affectionate dutifulness with which of late Judy treated her grandfather, she still showed her thorny side to Launcelot.

"Oh, well, of course, if you don't want to come" - she snapped, tartly, and went forward to meet the young people, who were hurrying up, Amelia puffing and out of breath, Nannie with her red curls flying, and Tommy laden with a parting gift of apples, an added burden for the martyred Perkins.

Far down the road the train whistled. Anne was surrounded by a little circle of sorrowing friends. Even Launcelot was in the group, and Judy and the Judge stood alone.

"How they love her," said Judy, with a little ache of envy in her heart.

"How she loves them," said the wise old Judge. "That is the secret, Judy."

Amelia had brought Anne a box of fudge, Nannie a handkerchief made by her own stubby and patient fingers, and Launcelot made her happy with a book of fairy-tales, worn as to cover, but with rich things within - a book of his that she had long coveted.

"By-by, little Anne," he said, with a brotherly pat on her shoulder. Then he shook hands with the Judge. "I hope you will have a fine time, sir," he said. Then as he and Judy stood together for a moment, he handed her something wrapped carefully in tissue-paper.

"These are for you," he said, a little awkwardly.

She unwound the paper and gave a little cry of delight.

"Violets, oh, Launcelot - how did you know I loved them?"

"Guessed it - you had them on your hat, and I liked that violet colored dress you wore."

"And they are so sweet and fragrant. Where could you get them this time of year?"

"In my little hothouse. I forced them for you."

But he did not tell her of the hours he had spent over them.

She was silent for a moment. "It was lovely of you," she said, at last, with a little flush and with a sweetness that she rarely revealed. "It was lovely of you - and I was so hateful just now."

She reached out her hand to him, and his grasp was hearty, reassuring. "It wouldn't seem natural if you and I didn't fuss a little, would it, Judy?" and then the train pulled in.

"All aboard!" shouted the conductor.

Anne and Judy went through the Pullman, and came out on the observation platform.

"Tell little grandmother to take good care of Belinda and Becky," called Anne, whose heart yearned for her pets.

"And all of you come and see me," cried Judy, hoping that she might win some of the love that was extended to Anne.

"We will," they cried, "we will."

"We will," echoed Launcelot, with his eyes on the violets pinned on Judy's gray coat, "we will if we have to sit up nights to do it."

A flutter of handkerchiefs, a blur of gray coat and red one, a trail of blue smoke, and the train was gone, and life to those left in Fairfax seemed suddenly a monotonous blank. As Launcelot turned away from the station, he ran into Dr. Grennell, who was rushing breathlessly up the steps.

"Has the train gone?" panted the minister.

"Yes."

Dr. Grennell wiped his heated forehead.

"I am sorry for that," he said, "I wanted especially to see the Judge."

He had a letter in his hand, and he stood looking at it perplexedly.

"To tell the truth, Launcelot," he began slowly, "I have something strange to tell the Judge, and I didn't want him to get away before I saw him. It isn't a thing to write about - and oh, why did I miss that train -"

Launcelot waited while the minister stared wistfully down the shining track.

"Look here, Launcelot," he asked, suddenly, "do you remember that Spanish coin of Judy's?"

"Well, I should say I did," replied the boy.

"It's the strangest thing - the strangest thing - oh, I'm going to tell you all about it, and see if you can help me out. Is there any place that we can be quite alone? I want to read this letter to you."

"There isn't a soul in the waiting-room," said Lancelot, "we can go in there. You'd better run on without me, Tommy," he called, "the doctor wants me. You can catch up with the girls if you hurry," and Tommy, who had eyed the pair with curiosity, departed crestfallen.

"I received this letter this morning," explained Dr. Grennell, as they sat down in the stuffy little room. "Read it. It's from an old friend of mine in Newfoundland - a physician."

The letter opened with personal matters, but the paragraph that the minister pointed out to Lancelot read thus:

"We have had a rather unusual case here lately. You know how often we have men brought to the hospital who have been shipwrecked, and as a rule there is little that is interesting about them - most of them are the type of ordinary seamen. Our latest case, however, was entered by the captain of a sailing vessel, who reported that they had picked the man up from a raft. That he was delirious then, and had never been able to tell them who he was or whence he came. He is still very ill and unconscious, and there is not a paper about him of identification. He is a gentlemen - I am sure of that, for his broken sentences are uttered in perfect English, and his hands tell it, too. As I have said, there isn't a letter or a paper about him, but around his neck on a silver chain we found the coin which I enclose. I know your fancy for odd coins, and so I send it, thinking perhaps you may give us some clue to our patient's identity."

Launcelot's eyes were bright with excitement as he finished reading.

"Let me see the coin," he begged, eagerly, and as the doctor handed it to him, he jumped to his feet.

"I thought so," he shouted, "it's a Spanish coin, like Judy's."

"Well," said the minister, quietly, but his hand beating against his knee showed that his agitation matched Launcelot's - "What then?"

"Why, the man must be Judy's father!" said Launcelot, and when he had thus voiced the doctor's thought, the two stared at each other with white faces.

"She always believed he was alive," said Launcelot at last.

"Pray God that it is really he?" said Dr. Grennell, reverently.

"And now what can we do?" asked the boy.

"We must not say a word to Judy yet. In fact I don't know whether we ought to tell the Judge. We musn't raise false hopes."

"Have you ever seen Captain Jameson?"

"We were at college together," said Dr. Grennell; "that is the way I happened to come to Fairfax. I got my appointment to this church through Captain Jameson and his father."

"Then couldn't you go on and see if he is really Judy's father?"

"By George," said the doctor, "of course I can. I can make the excuse that I want to visit my old friends. I need an outing, too."

"I wish I could go with you," said Launcelot, wistfully, as the two walked down the road, after having perfected plans for the doctor's trip. "I am getting awfully tired of this place, doctor. You see my life abroad was so different, and I feel as if I ought to be doing something worth while."

"Just now the thing that is worth while is for you to be a good son and stay here," said Dr. Grennell. "You can be nothing greater than that. And you are doing it like a hero," and his hand dropped affectionately on the boy's shoulder.

"Well, it's deadly dull," said the hero resignedly, as he thought of Anne and Judy speeding away to the coolness of the sea. But presently he cheered up. "It will be great if it does happen to be Captain Jameson," he said, "and just think if Judy hadn't run away we wouldn't have seen her coin, and if I had waited that morning she wouldn't have run away, and if I hadn't been cross I would have waited - how about that for a moral, Doctor."

"There is no moral," said the minister, "but all bad tempers don't turn out so well."

"It sounds like,

"'Fire, fire burn stick,
Stick, stick beat dog,
Dog, dog bite pig - '

doesn't it?" said Launcelot with a laugh, as they parted at the crossroads.

CHAPTER XVI

THE WIND AND THE WAVES

It was dark and raining when the travellers reached The Breakers, but a light streamed out from the doorway, and Mrs. Adams, the caretaker, met them on the step.

"I couldn't get any maids to help me," she explained to the Judge, as she led the way in, "but my sister is coming over in the morning, and Jim will build the fires - and I've set out supper in the hall."

"That's all right, Mrs. Adams," said the Judge, heartily, "Perkins will serve us, and you needn't stay up. I know you are tired after hurrying to get the house ready for us."

"Being tired ain't nothin' so that things suits," said Mrs. Adams, with an awed glance at the expert Perkins, who having relieved the Judge of his hat and raincoat was carrying the bags up-stairs under the guidance of Mr. Adams.

"Everything is just right, Mrs. Adams," said Judy, with eyes aglow. "I am so glad you set the supper-table in front of the big fireplace - we used to sit here so often."

Her voice trembled a little over the "we," for the sight of the little round table with its shining glass and silver had unnerved her. But she had made up her mind to be brave, and in a minute she was herself again, leading the way to her room, which Anne was to share, and doing the honors of the house generally.

The Breakers was a cottage built half of stone and half of shingles. It was roomy and comfortable, but not as magnificent as the Judge's great mansion in Fairfax. To Judy it was home, however, and when she came down again, she sighed blissfully as she dropped into a chair in front of the blazing fire.

"Listen, Anne," she said to the little fair-haired girl, "listen - do you hear them - the wind and the waves?"

Anne was not quite sure that she liked it - the moaning of the wind, and the ceaseless swish - boom, crash of the waves.

"I wish it was daylight so that I could see the ocean," she said, politely, "I think it must be lovely and blue and big -"

"It is lovely now," said Judy, and went to the window and drew back the curtain.

"Look out here, Anne -"

As Anne looked out, the moon showed for an instant in a ragged sky and lighted up a wild waste of waters, whose white edge of foam ran up the beach half-way to the cottage.

"How high the waves are," said little Anne.

"I have seen them higher than that," exulted Judy. "I have seen them so high that they seemed to tower above our roof."

"Weren't you afraid?"

"They couldn't hurt me, and it was grand."

"Supper is served, miss," announced Perkins, coming in with a chafing-dish and a half-dozen fresh eggs on a silver tray.

"I thought you might like something hot, sir," he said to the Judge with a supercilious glance at the cold collation which Mrs. Adams had provided, and with that he proceeded on the spot to make an omelette - puffy, fluffy, and perfect.

It was a cozy scene - the old butler in his white coat bending over the shining silver dish with the blue flame underneath. The polished mahogany of the table giving out rich reflections as the ruddy light of the fire played over it. The sparkling glass, the quaint old silver, Judy's violets all fragrant and dewy in the center, and at the head of the table the Judge in a great armchair, and on each side the two girls, the dark-haired and the fair-haired, in white gowns and crisp ribbons.

But Judy ate nothing, although Perkins tempted her with various offers.

"I'm not a bit hungry," she said, over and over again, and Anne, who was ravenous, felt positively greedy in the face of such daintiness.

"You are tired," said the Judge at last, as Judy sat with her chin in her hand, gazing at a picture of her father which hung over the fireplace - a full-length portrait in uniform. "Go to bed, dear." And in spite of protests, as soon as Anne had finished her supper, he ordered them both to bed.

"What are we going to do about her, Perkins?" the Judge asked in a worried tone, when he and the old servant were alone.

"Miss Judy, sir?"

"Yes. She isn't well, Perkins."

"She will be better down here, sir," said Perkins. "She is like her father, you know, sir - likes the water -"

"Perkins -" after a pause.

"Yes, sir."

"Do you think - he is alive?"

It was the first time in years that the Judge had spoken of his son. Perkins stopped brushing the crumbs from the table, and came and stood beside his master, looking into the fire thoughtfully.

"Miss Judy thinks he is, sir," he said at last.

"I know -"

"And I find that it's the women that's mostly right in such things," went on Perkins. "A man now only knows what he sees, but, Lord, sir, a woman knows things without seein'. Sort of takes them on faith, sir."

"The uncertainty is bad for Judy," said the Judge, the deep lines showing in his care-worn face.

Perkins laid a respectful hand on the back of his chair. "You'd best go to bed yourself; sir," he said, gently, "you're tired, sir."

"Yes - yes." But he did not move until Perkins had drawn the water for his bath and had laid out his things, and had urged him, "Everything is ready, sir." Then he got up with a sigh, "I wish I knew."

"I wish I knew," he said, a half-hour later, as the careful Perkins covered him with an extra blanket. "I wish I knew where he is - to-night."

Outside the wind moaned, the rain beat against the windows and the waves boomed unceasingly. Perkins drew the curtain tight, and laid the Judge's Bible on the little table by the bed, where his hand could reach it the first thing in the morning; then he picked up the lamp and went to the door.

"I think wherever he is, he's bein' took care of, sir," he said, comfortingly, and with an affectionate glance at the gray head on the pillow, he went out and closed the door.

In the morning Anne slept soundly, but Judy slipped out of bed early, put on her bathing-suit and a raincoat, and with a towel in her hand went down-stairs.

She found Perkins in the lower hall.

"You are early, Miss," he said.

"Yes, I am going to take a dip in the waves," said Judy.

"You're sure it's safe, Miss?" asked Perkins anxiously.

"I have done it all my life," asserted Judy, "and it gives me an awful appetite for breakfast."

Perkins brightened. "Does it now, Miss," he asked. "Is there anything you would like cooked, Miss Judy - I could speak to Mrs. Adams."

But Judy shook her head. "I am not hungry now," she said gaily, as she went off, "but I know I shall have an appetite when I come in."

She tripped away to the bath-house, and as she came out of the door looking like a sea-nymph in her white-bathing suit and white rubber cap she saw Anne, also towel laden and rain-coated, flying down towards her.

"Why didn't you wake me up," scolded the younger girl. "Oh, Judy, isn't it lovely," and she dropped down on the beach, panting.

The morning sun cast rosy shadows over the sea, there was a touch of amethyst in the clouds, and the waves as they curled over the golden beach were gray-green in the hollows and silver-white on their crests.

"I just know I sha'n't dare to stick my toes into the water," said Anne with a shiver. "It is so - so big, Judy."

"You look just dear," declared Judy, as Anne dropped her raincoat and came forth in a scarlet suit, "that red suits you."

Anne clasped her hands. "Oh, Judy, does it," she sighed rapturously.

"Yes."

"You don't think I am getting vain, do you, Judy?" inquired Anne, anxiously, "but I do love pretty things."

"I think you are a goosie," said Judy with a little laugh, then she caught hold of Anne with impatient hands. "Come on in, little red bird," she urged, "it's lovely in the water."

Anne squealed and struggled, and finally waded in until the water came up to her knees.

"Don't take me any farther, Judy," she begged, and when Judy saw her frightened face, she let her go.

"Sit on the sand, then, and watch me, Annekins," she advised. "You will get used to this after a while and enjoy it as much as I do."

She was off with a run and a leap, and for fifteen minutes or more she was over and under and up and down on the waves like a snowy mermaid.

"And now for breakfast," said the young lady in white, as she dashed up the sands, with raincoat flying and towel fluttering in the breeze.

Ten minutes later two red-cheeked, wet-haired damsels rushed into the dining-room and kissed the Judge, who sat at the head of the table with his newspaper propped up in front of him.

"Bless my soul," he said, gazing at them over his spectacles, "are you really up?"

"We have been up for an hour," gurgled Anne, happily, "and in bathing."

But Judy did not stop for explanations, "Oh, waffles, waffles. Perkins, I love you. How did you know I wanted waffles?"

"You said you would have an appetite, Miss," said the beaming Perkins, "and there's nothing that touches the spot on a cool morning like waffles."

He exchanged satisfied glances with the Judge as Judy finished her sixth section, having further supplemented the waffles with a dish of berries and a lamb chop.

"We are going down to the bay after breakfast," announced Judy.

"And I am going to take a book and read on the sand," planned Anne.

"Books, nothing," said Judy, slangily. "We are going to sail and catch crabs."

"Little red crabs?" asked Anne with interest.

"No, big blue ones, you goosie, and then Perkins will cook them for us. Won't you, Perkins?"

"Anything you say, Miss," said Perkins, resignedly.

But it rained the next day, and after that they went sailing in Judy's own sailboat "The Princess," which she could manage as well as any man, and after that they drove to town with the

Judge, so that it was over a week before the crabbing expedition came to pass.

The Breakers stood on a strip of land between the bay and the ocean. It was on a peninsula, but the connecting link with the mainland was many miles away, so that for all practical purposes the house was on an island, with the ocean in front and the bay behind, and all the pleasures that both made possible.

Anne was entranced with the delights of crabbing. It was very exciting to get the great rusty fellows on the line, tow them up to the top of the water, where the competent Perkins nabbed them with the crab-net.

Perkins caught crabs as he did everything else, expertly, and with dignity. His only concession to the informality of the sport was a white yachting cap and a white linen coat, and it was a sight worth going miles to see, to watch him officiate at a catch. The great vicious fellows might clash their claws in vain, for Perkins subdued them with a scientific clutch at the back that rendered them helpless.

"We are going to cook them as soon as we get home," Judy told Anne. "Perkins knows all about fixing them, and Mrs. Adams is going to give up the kitchen to us - it's lots of fun to eat the meat out of the claws."

"Do you want them - devilled, Miss?" and Perkins coughed discreetly before the word.

"Yes. In their shells, with parsley stuck in the top. They are delicious that way, Anne."

Anne had her doubts as to the deliciousness of anything so spidery-looking as those strange fish, but she said nothing.

"Is there anything Perkins can't do?" she asked Judy, as Perkins went on ahead, bearing the great basket of crabs, and the net.

"I don't believe there is," laughed Judy. "He is supposed to be grandfather's butler, but he won't let any one do a thing for grandfather, and he plays valet and cook half the time when the other servants don't suit him."

Once in the kitchen, Anne eyed the big basket shiveringly. The fierce creatures stared at her with protruding bead-like eyes, and in a way that seemed positively menacing.

"If they should get out," she thought, as she was left alone with them for a moment.

She never knew how it happened, but Perkins must have left the basket too near the edge of the chair on which he had placed it, for as she took hold of the cover to shut it, the basket tipped, and down came the living load, and in another moment, the desperate shell-fish were scuttling across the floor in all directions.

With a shriek Anne took refuge on top of the stationary wash-tubs.

"Come up here, Judy," she cried, frantically, and Judy who had reached the middle of the room, and was surrounded by pugilistic creatures before she realized the catastrophe, drew herself up beside Anne, and together they shrieked for Perkins.

Perkins came and saw and conquered as usual. The girls laughed until the tears ran down their cheeks to see the battle. One by one the crabs were picked up and dropped into a big kettle until at last it was full.

"And now you young ladies had best go out," said Perkins, firmly, "while I cook them."

It is well to draw a veil over the tragic fate of the kettleful of blue crabs, but when Anne next saw them they were beautifully boiled, and red - red as the scarlet of her bathing-suit.

All the afternoon the little girls, under Perkins' skilful guidance learned a lesson in expert cookery, and at last, as a dozen perfectly browned and parsley-decorated beauties were laid on a platter, Judy breathed an ecstatic sigh. "Aren't they beautiful?" she murmured.

"Yes, Miss, that they are," and Perkins surveyed them as an artist lets his glance linger on a finished masterpiece. He raised the platter to carry it to the dining-room, but as he turned towards the door he stopped and set it down quickly.

"What's the matter, sir," he asked sharply, "has anything gone wrong?"

The Judge stood on the threshold, his face white with excitement. In his hands was a letter, and his voice shook as he spoke.

"It's nothing bad, Perkins," he said, and Judy, as she faced him, saw that his eyes were bright with some new hope. "It's nothing bad. But I've had a letter - a strange, strange letter, Perkins - and I must go on a journey to-night - a journey to the north - to Newfoundland, Perkins."

CHAPTER XVII

MOODS AND MODELS

Anne and Judy were almost overcome by the mystery of the Judge's departure. Not a word could they get out of the reticent Perkins, however, as to the reasons for the sudden flitting, and the Judge had simply said when pressed with questions: "Important business, my dear, which may result rather pleasantly for you. Mrs. Adams will take care of you and Anne while I am gone, which I hope won't be long."

The day that he left it rained, and the day after, and the day after that, and on the fourth day, when the sea was gray and the sky was gray and the world seemed blotted out by the blinding torrents, Judy, who had been pacing through the house like a caged wild thing, came into the library, and found Anne curled up in the window-seat with a book.

"I came down here with all sorts of good resolutions," she said, fiercely, as she stood by the window, looking out, "but if this rain doesn't stop, I shall do something desperate. I hate to be shut in."

Anne did not look up. She was reading a book breathlessly, and not until Judy had jerked it out of her hand and had flung it across the room did she come to herself with a little cry.

"I shall do something desperate," reiterated Judy, stormily. "Do you hear, Anne?"

Anne smiled up at her - a preoccupied smile.

"Oh, Judy," she said, still seeing the visions conjured up by her book. "Oh, Judy, you ought to read this -"

"You know I don't like to read, Anne." Judy's tone was irritable.

"You would like this," said Anne, gently, as she drew Judy down beside her. "It's about the sea." She opened the despised book at the place where she had been reading when Judy plucked it out of her hand. "Listen."

Judy did listen, but with her sullen eyes staring out of the window and her shoulders hunched up aggressively. When Anne stopped however, she said: "Go on," and when the chapter was finished, she asked, "Who wrote that?"

"Robert Louis Stevenson. He was a lovely man, and he wrote lovely books, and he died, and they buried him in Samoa on the top of a mountain. He wrote some verses called 'Requiem.' I think you would like them, Judy."

"What are they?"

Anne quoted softly, her sweet little voice deep with feeling, and her blue eyes dark with emotion.

"'Under the wide and stormy sky,
Dig the grave and let me lie,
Glad did I live and gladly die,
And I laid me down with a will.

"'This be the verse you grave for me:
"Here he lies where he longed to be;
Home is the sailor - home from the sea,
And the hunter home from the hill."'"

"'Home is the sailor, home from the sea -'" echoed Judy,

under her breath. "How fine that he could say it like that, Anne. Tell me about him."

All the discontent had gone from her face, and she lay back among the cushions of the window-seat quietly, while Anne told her of the young life that had ended in a land of exile. Of a singer whose song had been stilled so soon, but who would not be forgotten as long as men honor a brave heart and a gentle spirit.

"Let me see the book," and Judy stretched out her hand, and Anne gave her "Kidnapped" unselfishly, glad to see the softened look in Judy's eyes, and as the morning passed and the two girls read on and on, they did not notice that the rain had stopped and that the parted clouds showed a gleam of watery sun.

And when lunch was announced, Judy laid her book down with a sigh, and after lunch, in spite of clearing weather, she read until twilight, and having finished one book, would have started another, if Anne had not protested.

"You will wear yourself out," she said, as the intense Judy looked up with blurred eyes and wrinkled forehead. "Let's have a run on the beach."

Judy never did anything by halves, and after her introduction to books that she liked, she outread Anne. And as time went on it was her books that soothed her in her restless moods, and because there were in her father's library the writings of the greatest men and the best men who have given their thoughts to the world, Judy was gradually molded into finer girlhood, finer womanhood, than could have come to her by any other association.

She read Stevenson through in a week, and then began on Ruskin; for her thoughtful mind, starved so long of food that it needed, craved solid things, and Judy, who knew much of pictures and paintings, found in Ruskin's theories a great deal that delighted and interested her.

"You'll never get through," said Anne, with a dismayed glance at the long rows of brown volumes high up on the shelves. "I don't like anything but stories, and Ruskin preaches awfully."

"You ought to like him, then," said Judy, wickedly, "you good little Anne."

"Oh, don't," protested Anne, reproachfully, "don't call me that, Judy."

"Well, bad little Anne, then," said Judy, composedly, from the top of the step-ladder, where she was examining the titles of the books and enjoying herself generally.

"You're such a tease," said Anne with a sigh.

"And you are so serious, little Annekins," and Judy smiled down at her.

"I like Ruskin," she announced, later. "He's a little hard to understand sometimes, but he knows a lot about art. I am going to take up my drawing again. He says that youth is the time to do things, and a girl ought not to fritter away her time."

"No, indeed," said Anne, virtuously. "Only don't get too tired, Judy."

But it was Anne who was tired, before Judy's enthusiasm wore itself out, for she was pressed into service as a model, and she served in turn as A Blind Girl, A Dancing Girl, A Greek Maiden, Rebecca at the Well, Marguerite, and Lorelei.

The last was an inspiration. Anne perched on a rock around which the breakers dashed appropriately, with her hair down, and with filmy garments fluttering in the wind, combed her golden locks in the heat of the blazing sun.

"It's broiling hot out here, Judy," she complained as that indefatigable artist sat on the beach with her easel before her, in a blue work-apron, and with a dab of charcoal on her nose.

"Oh, you look just lovely, Anne," Judy assured her, with the cruel indifference of genius. "You're just lovely. I think this is the best I have done yet. Think what a picture you will make."

"Think how my nose will peel," mourned Anne, forlornly.

> "Die schoenste Jungfrau sitzet
> Dort oben wunderbar,
> Ihr goldnes Geschmeide blitzet,
> Sie kaemmt ihr gold'nes Haar."

sang Judy, whose residence abroad had made her familiar with many folk-songs.

> Sie kaemmt es mit gold'nem Kamme,
> Und singt ein Lied dabei;"

"- Anne, you have the loveliest hair," she interrupted her song to say.

But Anne was tired. "I don't think that the Lorelei was very nice," she said, "to make men drown themselves just because she wants to comb her hair on a rock -"

"She didn't care," said Judy, sagely. "The men didn't have to let their old boats be wrecked."

"But her voice was so wonderful they just had to follow -"

"No, they didn't," declared Judy. "You just ask your grandmother. She says nobody has to go where they don't want to go, and I think she is right, and if those sailors had sailed away the minute they heard the Lorelei begin to sing they would have been safe."

"Well, maybe they would," agreed Anne, hastily, for Judy had stopped work to talk. "Judy, I shall fall off this rock if you don't finish pretty soon."

"All right, Annekins, just one minute," and Judy dashed in a drowning sailor or two, fluffed the heroine's hair into entrancing curliness, added a few extra rays to the sparkling comb, and held up the sketch.

"There," she said, triumphantly.

Anne slid from the rock, and waded in to look.

"It isn't a bit like me," she criticized, holding up her wet and flowing draperies.

"Well, you see I couldn't put in your dimples and your chubbiness, for although they are dear in you, Anne, they are not suitable for the purposes of art," and Judy stood back with a grown-up air and gazed upon her masterpiece. Then she caught Anne around the waist and danced with her on the beach.

"Ich glaube, die Wellen verschlingen
Am Ende Schiffer und Kahn;
Und das hat mit ihrem Singen
Die Lorelei gethan."

"You wicked little Lorelei," she panted, as they sat down on the sand.

"I'm not wicked," said Anne, composedly, "and the next time you use me for a model, Judy, I wish you would get an easier place than on that old rock."

"You shall be Juliet in the tomb," promised Judy, "and you can go to sleep if you want to."

But she let Anne rest for awhile, and used Perkins as a model.

Her first sketch of him was very clever - a sketch in which the stately butler posed as "The Neptune of the Kitchen." He sat on a great turtle, with a toasting-fork instead of a trident, with a necklace of oyster crackers, a crown of pickles, and a smile that was truly Perkins's own.

That sketch taught Judy her niche in the temple of art. She was not destined to be a great artist, but she had a keen wit, and a knack of discovering fun in everything, and in later years it was in caricature, not unkind, but truly humorous, that Judy made her greatest successes, and achieved some little fame.

CHAPTER XVIII

JUDY KEEPS A PROMISE

"What's your talent, Anne?" asked Judy, one evening, as she lay on the couch reading "Sesame and Lilies." It was raining again outside, but in the fireplace a great fire was blazing, and rosy little Anne was in front of it, popping corn.

"Haven't any," said Anne, watching the white kernels bob up and down. "I can't draw and I can't play, and I can't sing or converse - or anything."

Judy looked at her thoughtfully. "Well, we will have to find something that you can do," she said, for Judy liked to lead and have others follow, and having decided upon art as her life-work, she wanted Anne to choose a similar path. "I wish I could take up bookbinding or wood-carving, or - or dentistry -"

"Why, Judy Jameson." Anne turned an amazed hot face towards her. "Why, Judy, you wouldn't like to pull teeth, would you?"

"It isn't what we like to do, Ruskin says," said Judy, calmly, "it's usefulness that counts."

"Oh, well, I can wash dishes and dust and take care of old people and pets," said placid Anne, opening the cover of the popper and letting out delicious whiffs of hot corn.

Judy shuddered. "I hate those things," she said. "I couldn't wash dishes, Anne. It is so dreadful for your hands."

She went back to her book, and Anne poured the hot corn into a big bowl and salted it.

"Have some?" she asked the absorbed reader.

Without taking her eyes from her book, Judy stretched out her hand, then all at once she flashed a glance into the rosy face so close to her own.

"Anne," she said, almost humbly, "do you know you are more of a Ruskin girl than I am? He says that every girl, every day, should do something really useful about the house - go into the kitchen, and sew, and learn how to fold table-cloths, and things, like that. And you know all of those things - and how to help the poor - and I - I am always trying to do some great thing, and I never really help any one. Not any one, Anne - not a single soul -"

"But you are so clever," said little Anne.

"But people don't love you just because you are clever, and it isn't clever people that make others the happiest," and Judy dropped her book and gazed deep into the flames as if seeking there an answer to the problems of life.

"People love you, Judy."

"Sometimes they do, and some people - but my awful temper, Anne," and Judy sighed.

"You don't flare up half as much as you used." Anne's tone was consoling. She had finished popping the corn, and she sat down on the floor beside the couch on which Judy lay, and munched the crisp kernels luxuriously.

"No, I don't," confessed Judy, "but it's an awful fight, Anne.

You have helped me a lot."

"Me?" asked the rosy maiden in astonishment. "Why, how have I helped you, Judy?"

"By your example, Annekins," said Judy, sitting up. "You're such a dear."

At which praise the rosy maiden got rosier than ever, and shook her loosened hair over her happy eyes.

The firelight flickered on the beautiful dark face on the cushions, and on the fair little one that rested against Judy's dress.

"We are such friends, aren't we, Judy?" whispered Anne, as she reached up and curled her plump hand into Judy's slender fingers. "Almost like sisters, aren't we, Judy?"

"Just like sisters, Annekins," said Judy, dreamily, with a responsive pressure.

Outside the wind moaned and groaned, and the rain beat against the panes. "I have never seen such a rainy season," said Judy, as a blast shook the house. "But I rather like it when we are so cozy and warm and happy, Anne."

The pop-corn was all eaten, and Anne was gazing into the fire, half asleep, when suddenly she started up.

"What's that, Judy?" she cried.

Judy raised her eyes from her book.

"What?" she asked, abstractedly.

"That sound at the window."

"I didn't hear anything."

"It was like a rap."

"It was the rain."

"Well, maybe it was," and Anne settled back again. Presently her hand slipped and dropped, and Judy, feeling the movement, looked down and smiled, for little Anne was asleep.

Judy tucked a cushion behind the weary head, and was settling back for another quiet hour with her book, when all at once she sat up straight, listening.

Then she rolled from the couch quickly, without waking Anne, and went to the window and peered out. She could see nothing but the driving rain, but as she turned to leave there came again the sound that had startled her.

The window was a French one, opening outward. Very softly she unlatched it.

"Who's there?" she asked, wondering if she should have called Perkins.

"Come to the door," said a voice, and a dripping figure appeared within the circle of light. "Come out a minute. It's me - Tommy Tolliver."

Anne slept on as Judy went out and closed the door behind her.

"Why, Tommy," she said, trying to see him in the darkness, "how in the world did you get down here?"

"I have run away again," said Tommy, defiantly, "and I've come to you to help me, Judy."

"What!"

"You said you would help me, Judy. That's why I came."

"But -"

"Oh, don't try to get out of it," blazed Tommy, who was wet and tired and shivering, "you said you would. And if you back down now - well -" He left the sentence unfinished and his voice broke.

"*When* did I promise, Tommy?" asked poor Judy, in a dazed way.

"The day I came back to Fairfax."

It seemed like a dream to Judy, that day in the woods when she had first met the children of Fairfax, - Launcelot and Amelia and Nannie, - and she had entirely forgotten her reckless promise.

"Sit down," she faltered, "and tell me what you want me to do."

At the side of the house where they were sheltered somewhat from the rain Tommy outlined his plan.

"I want you to take me down the bay in your sailboat. I had money enough to get here, and if you can help me to get to the Point, a friend of mine has promised me a place on one of the ocean liners."

"But Tommy -"

"Don't say 'but' to me, Judy," and Judy recognized a new note in Tommy's voice. There was less of the old, weak swagger, and more determination. "I am going, and that's all there is to it."

"When do you want to start?" she asked, after a pause.

"The first thing in the morning, if you can get away," said Tommy.

"I can't go until evening. We are to spend the day with some friends of ours, the Bartons. But I can take you down by moonlight. It's a couple of hours' ride. I suppose we shall have to tell Anne."

"I hate to," said Tommy.

"Why?"

"Oh, Anne is such a good little thing - and - and - she believes in me - Judy."

"But if it is right for you to go, you shouldn't care -"

"I don't know whether it is right or not," said Tommy, doggedly, "and what's more, I don't care, Judy. I am going and that's the end of it."

"Well!" Judy stood up, shivering. "It's awfully cold out here, Tommy; you'd better come in."

"Are you going to help me?" demanded Tommy. "I sha'n't go in unless you are."

"What will you do?"

"Tramp on. Guess I can manage for another day. I've only had a slice of bread and a tomato to-day."

"Tommy Tolliver!" said Judy, shocked. "Why, you must be starved. I'll go right in and get you something."

"Are you going to help me to get away?" he insisted.

"I must think about it."

"But you promised."

"I am not sure that I exactly promised," hesitated Judy.

"You're afraid."

"I am not."

"Aw, you are - or you'd do it."

That was touching Judy on a tender point. She was proud of her courage - none of her race had ever been cowards.

Besides, as she stood there with the wind and the waves beating their wild song into her ears, all the recklessness of her nature came uppermost. It would be glorious to sail down the bay. The water would be rough, and the wind would fill out the white sails of the little boat, and they would fly, fly, and the goal for Tommy would be freedom.

"I'll do it," she said, suddenly. "I'll do it, Tommy. We Jamesons never break a promise, and I'm not afraid."

They decided not to tell Anne.

"It would just worry her," said Judy, decidedly, "and I can get some food and things out to you after Anne goes to bed, and you can sleep in the boat-house. We can start in the morning."

It was a wild scheme, but before they had finished they felt quite uplifted. In their youth and inexperience, they imagined that Tommy's last dash for liberty was positively heroic, and Judy went in, feeling like one dedicated to a cause.

She found Anne rubbing her eyes sleepily.

"Why, have you been out, Judy?" she gasped, wide awake. "You are all wet."

"It's fine on the porch," said Judy, putting her soaked hair back from her face. "I - I was tired of the heat of the room, and - it was stifling. Let's go to bed, Anne."

"Aren't you going to finish your book?" Anne asked, wondering, for Judy was something of a night-owl, and hated early hours.

Judy picked up "Sesame and Lilies," which lay open on the couch, and shut it with a bang.

"No," she said, shortly, "I am not going to finish it to-night - I don't know whether I shall ever finish it, Anne. I'm not Ruskin's kind of girl, Anne. I can't 'sit on a cushion and sew a fine seam,' and I don't think it is any use for me to try."

Anne stared at the change that had come over her. "Well, you are my kind of girl," she said at last, and as they went up-stairs together, she slipped her hand into Judy's arm. "I love you, dearly, Judy," she said.

But Judy smiled down at her vaguely, for her mind was on Tommy, crouched out there in the rain, and in imagination she was not Judy Jameson, commonplacely going to bed at nine o'clock, but a heroine of history, dedicated to the cause of one Thomas, the Downtrodden.

CHAPTER XIX

PERKINS CLEANS THE SILVER

All the next day, Tommy skulked in the shadow of the pier and in the boat-house, whence during the morning Judy made her way laden with mysterious bundles and various baggage. At noon she departed for Lutie Barton's, leaving Anne, who had a cold, at home.

After Judy's departure, Anne wandered listlessly about the house. She tried to read, to sew a little, to pick out some simple tunes on Judy's piano, but thoughts of the little gray house, of the little grandmother, of Becky and Belinda, came between her and her occupations, so that at last, late in the afternoon, she sought the society of Perkins, who was in the dining-room cleaning silver.

"I believe I am homesick, Perkins," said Anne, perching herself in a great mahogany chair opposite him.

"Well, it ain't to be wondered at," said Perkins, as he picked up a huge cake-dish and began to work on it, energetically. "It ain't to be wondered at. You ain't ever been away from home much, Miss Anne."

"It is lovely not to have anything to do," said Anne. "That is, it is nice in a way, but do you know, Perkins, I sometimes just wish there were some rooms to dust or something, but you and the maids keep everything so clean," and Anne sighed a sigh that came from the depths of her housewifely soul.

"You might dip these cups in hot water and wipe them as I gets them finished," suggested Perkins, handing her several quaint little mugs, which he had placed in a row in front of him.

"Aren't they dear," Anne said, enthusiastically. "Why this one says 'Judith.' Is it Judy's, Perkins?"

"No, Miss, that was her great-grand-mother's, and that one with 'John' on it is the Judge's, and the one with 'Philip' is Miss Judy's father's - they are christening cups, Miss - six generations of them."

"Oh, how lovely," said Anne, and she handled them lovingly, dipping them into clear hot water, and polishing them until they shone.

"Judy never speaks of her father, lately," she said, as she placed the "Philip" cup on the sideboard.

"No, Miss, but she thinks of him a lot," said Perkins, with a shake of his old head. "I saw her this morning, Miss, standing in front of his picture in the hall, and there were tears in her eyes, Miss, and then all at once she whirled around and ran away, and her face had a wild look on it, Miss."

"Do you know, Perkins," said little Anne, stopping work for a minute and speaking earnestly, "do you know that I think Judy would be different if she only knew something about him. The uncertainty makes her unhappy, and then she does reckless things just to get away from herself."

"Yes, Miss," said Perkins, "and there ain't a morning that she don't put fresh flowers in front of that there picture, and there ain't a night that she don't kiss her hand to it from the top of the stairs."

"I know," sighed Anne. "Poor Judy."

"When will the Judge be back?" she asked after awhile.

But at that Perkins shut up like a clam. "I don't know, Miss," he snapped. "It's best for you not to ask too many questions, Miss."

Anne flushed. "Oh, of course I won't, Perkins," she said, "if you don't like to have me -" and she was very quiet, until the old butler, with a glance at her troubled face, said, "I don't care how many questions you axes, Miss, but the Judge might."

And Anne smiled at him, with radiant forgiveness.

"Isn't all this silver a lot of care, Perkins?" she asked, to clear the air.

"It is that," answered Perkins, "and yet there isn't half as much of it as there is at the Judge's in Fairfax. Only the Judge keeps his locked up in a safe, all except the things we uses every day. But here they just puts it on the sideboard, where it is a temptation to burglars - with them long windows opening out on the porch, and the curtains drawn back half the time. I don't call it safe, Miss, I surely don't."

"But there aren't any burglars around here, are there, Perkins?" and Anne stopped rubbing the cups to look at him anxiously.

"Nobody knows whether there is or not," grumbled Perkins. "There might be for all they know. It ain't fair to the servants, Miss, for to let them lie around loose this way. Mrs. Adams says so, too, but the Judge don't pay no attention to things since the Captain left, and Miss Judy is too young to bother."

"They wouldn't like to lose these cups," said Anne, as she finished the last one, and arranged them in a squat little row on the shelf.

"They wouldn't like to lose any of it," returned Perkins, putting a great soup-ladle back into its flannel bag. "It's all old and it's all family silver, and people ought to take care of it, and when the Judge comes back I am going to tell him so, Miss."

"Anne," said Judy, peeping in at the door, "I'm back, and Lutie Barton is with me. Come on in and see her."

"Oh, dear," said Anne, with a dismayed glance at her spattered apron, "I look like a sight."

"Run up the back way and fix up," said Judy, "and I'll talk to her until you come down."

Lutie Barton brought with her the gossip of the town. There had been a dance at the big hotel the night before, a sailing party down the bay in the afternoon had been caught in a thunder shower, and all the girls' hats had been ruined, and there had been a burglary at one of the cottages in an outlying district.

Anne jumped when they said that. "What did they steal?" she faltered, with her conversation with Perkins fresh in her mind.

"*Everything*, my dear," said Lutie, who did everything by extremes, and who wore the highest pompadour, and the highest heels, and who had the smallest waist and the largest hat that Anne had ever seen, and who always used the superlative when telling a tale.

"They stole *every single thing* down to the very shoes, and the kitten from the rug."

"Oh," said Anne, thinking of Belinda, "the dear little kitten. What did they want with it?"

"It was a Persian, and this morning it came back, but the silver collar was gone from its neck, and they took even a thimble from a work-basket, and a box of candy and a cake!"

"Did they get anything valuable?" asked Anne.

"All of Mrs. Durant's diamonds and the family silver," said Lutie. "My dear, Mrs. Durant is ill, *absolutely ill,* and the worst of it is that she saw the burglar, and it frightened her so that she hasn't gotten over it yet."

"How dreadful," said little Anne, thinking of the great sideboard and all of the Jameson silver that she and Perkins had cleaned. "Oh, Judy, suppose they should come here!"

But Judy was standing by the window, watching a figure that slipped from the boat-house to the wharf with a bundle on his shoulder, the figure of a small boy, with his cap pulled low.

"Such things are like lightning; they never strike twice in the same place," she said, indifferently. "Don't go, Lutie."

"Oh, I *must,*" gushed Lutie. "I was just *dying* to see you, Anne, for a minute, so I came with Judy. But I *must* go. They will think I am *dead.*"

But she stopped to ask a giggling question. "Tell me about Launcelot Bart, Anne," she begged. "Judy happened to mention him, but she wouldn't tell me a *thing.* I think they must have an *awful* case, for she is too quiet about him for *anything.* Is he nice?"

"He is the nicest boy I know," said Anne, enthusiastically.

"Oh, oh," gurgled silly Lutie, shaking her finger at the two girls as they stood together on the top step of the porch. "Don't get jealous of each other, you two."

"Jealous?" asked Anne's innocent eyes.

"Jealous?" blazed Judy's indignant eyes.

"Don't be a goose, Lutie." Judy was trying to control her temper. "Anne and I aren't grown up yet, and I hope we never will grow up and be horrid and self-conscious. Launcelot is our friend, and I didn't talk about him because I had plenty of other subjects."

"Oh," murmured Lutie, subdued for the moment; but she recovered as she went down the walk. "Oh, *good-bye*," she gushed; "let me know when it is to be, and I will dance at your wedding."

"Anne," said Judy, darkly, as the high heels tilted down the beach, and the feathers of the big hat fluttered in the breeze, "Anne, she hasn't talked a thing to-day but boys - and she reads the silliest books and writes the silliest poetry, about flaming hearts and Cupid's darts. Oh," and Judy stretched out her arms in a tense movement, "I don't want to grow up - I want to stay a little girl as long as I can and not think about lovers or getting married, or - or - anything -"

"You are lover enough for me," said Anne.

"And you for me," said Judy.

And arm in arm they went into the house. But as they went through the darkening hall, Anne clung tightly to Judy.

"Wouldn't it be dreadful, Judy, if burglars should come here," she quavered.

But Judy laughed. "I think it would be fun," she jested. "Bring on your burglars, Anne. I'm *dying* for excitement, as Lutie Barton would say." And then she touched a button, and the lights flared up, chasing away the shadows, and chasing away with them, for the moment, the fears of little Anne.

CHAPTER XX

ANNE HEARS A BURGLAR

Anne was wakened that night by a sense of utter loneliness.

"Judy," she called, softly.

No answer.

"Judy."

Anne reached over and found that the covers of the little white bed that stood beside her own had not been disturbed.

"She hasn't come up-stairs," thought Anne, who had left Judy reading in the library when she went to bed.

There was no light in the room, and as little Anne lay there, trembling and listening, her breath came quickly, for she was a timid little soul, and the talk of burglars that day had upset her; and without the wind howled, and within the house was very, very still.

At last she heard a sound. "She's coming," she thought, thankfully, but all at once she became conscious that the sound was not in the upper hall, but down-stairs on the porch.

There was the quick patter of little feet, and then an appealing whine.

"Why, it's a dog," said Anne, sitting up straight, "It's a dog."

She got up and looked out of the window. A little short-eared, stubby-tailed Boston terrier was running back and forth on the sand, anxiously.

Anne was a tender-hearted lover of animals, and his apparent distress appealed to her.

"I'll go down and see what's the matter with him," she decided, thrusting her feet into her slippers and tying the ribbons of her pink dressing-gown.

She flew down the long dark hall to the top of the steps that led below, and there she stopped still, with her hand on her heart.

The fire in the hall was still burning, and the flames wavered fitfully over the great picture above the mantel, and on the jar of red roses in front of it. The rest of the hall was in the shadow, and darker than the shadows, Anne had made out the figure of a man standing on the threshold.

As she gazed, he crossed the room and stood in front of the fire, his eyes raised to the great picture. Suddenly he leaned forward and took one of the red roses from the jar.

"He is even stealing the roses," thought Anne, indignantly, but then, what could you expect of a man who would carry off boxes of candy and thimbles and kittens?

She was sure it was the Durant burglar, and she dropped to the floor cautiously, and crouched there. Outside she could still hear the whine of the dog, but she had no thought of going to him now - she could not pass that silent figure on the rug.

Then, all at once, she thought of Judy. She was in the library, and there was just one room between her and the burglar!

Anne wasn't brave, and never had been, but in that moment she forgot herself, forgot everything but that Judy was not well and must not be frightened at any cost. Judy must not see the burglar.

As the man moved across the hall Anne staggered to her feet, feeling along the wall for the electric button, and then suddenly the lights flared up, and the little girl, a desperate pink figure clinging to the stair-rail, looked down into the upraised face of the man below.

"Don't," she said, with white lips, "don't - go - in - there -"

As she stared at him in a blur of fright she was conscious of wondering if all burglars looked so gentlemanly - if - why, *where had she seen his face?*

"Judy," breathed the man, and his whisper seemed to thunder in her ears as he came up the stairway two steps at a time.

Anne gave a little scream, half fright, half delight.

"Oh -" Why, his face was familiar - it was the face of the man in the picture over the fireplace!

"Judy," he said, again, as he reached her and caught her in his arms. But as her yellow hair flowed over his coat, he laughed excitedly and put her from him. "I beg pardon," he apologized. "I thought you were Judy."

"And I thought you were a burglar," quavered Anne, as she sat down on the top step weakly.

Her fair little face was alight with joy as she held out her hand. "Oh," she said, "you are Judy's father, and you are alive, you are really alive!"

"And you are Anne," said the Captain.

"How did you know?" wondering.

"The Judge told me."

"Where did you see the Judge?" she asked.

"He has been with me ever since he left here," said the Captain. "Dr. Grennell discovered me in a hospital in Newfoundland, and I was very ill, and he sent for father, and he has been with me ever since. And he has gone straight to Fairfax, for he isn't very well. But I had to see my girl. Did I wake you?"

"I heard the dog."

"Terry? I brought him to Judy, and left him outside so he wouldn't startle the house. Where is my girl - where is she, Anne?"

"Oh, she's in the library," said Anne. "I'll call her. Oh, how happy she will be! How happy she will be!" She sang it like a little song, as she flitted through the hall.

At the same moment the electric bell of the front door thrilled through the house, and the Captain opened the door quickly.

Preceded by a blast of wind, and the scurrying Terry-dog, Launcelot Bart came in. He stood irresolute as he saw the strange man on the rug, and before either could speak, Anne came running back.

Her face was white and her hands were shaking. She did not seem to see Launcelot, but went straight up to Captain Jameson.

"Oh, where is Judy, where is Judy?" she wailed, "she isn't there."

"And where is Tommy Tolliver?" demanded Launcelot Bart.

CHAPTER XXI

CAPTAIN JUDY

"Gee, Judy, but you can sail a boat."

Judy with the salt breeze blowing her hair back from her face, with her hand on the tiller, and with her eager eyes sweeping the surface of the moonlighted waters, smiled a little.

"I ought to," she declared, "father taught me. He said that he didn't have a son, so he intended that I should know as much as a boy about such things."

"It's mighty windy weather." Tommy was hunched up in the bottom of the boat - and his face had the woebegone look of the inexperienced sailor.

"It's going to be windier," said Judy, wisely, "it's coming now. Look at those clouds."

Back of the moon a heavy bank of clouds was crested with white, and the waters of the bay heaved sullenly.

Tommy, ignorant little landlubber that he was, began to wish that he had stayed at home, but Judy was exalted, uplifted by the thought of a coming battle with wind and waves. She had fought them so often in the little white boat, but one thing she forgot, that she was not as strong as she had been, and that Tommy was not as helpful as her father.

The start had been very exciting. Judy had pretended to read in the library, and little Anne had gone to bed, and then when the house was still she had crept out, and had met Tommy, and together they had gotten "The Princess" under sail.

But more than once that day Judy's heart had failed her. The Cause had looked rather silly on second thoughts, and Tommy was *so* commonplace - but, oh, well, she had promised, and that was the end of it.

Tommy was dreadfully awkward about a boat, too. In spite of his eagerness for a life on the ocean wave, he had never had any practical training and Judy grew impatient more than once at the slow way in which he followed out her orders.

"I would do it myself," she scolded finally, "only I must save my strength for the trip back. I shall be all alone then, you know."

Tommy sat down suddenly. "Gracious," he gasped, "I never thought of that. Oh, we will have to go back. You can't take this boat home alone, Judy."

Judy's head went up. "I am captain of this ship, Tommy Tolliver," she declared, "and I am going to sail into port and put you ashore. Then I shall do as I like."

"Aw -" said Tommy, appalled at this display of nautical knowledge, "aw - all right, Captain Judy."

The wind came as Judy had said it would, filling the little sail until it looked like a white flower, and carrying "The Princess" along at a pace that made Tommy feel weak and faint.

"Isn't it fine," cried Judy, leaning forward, and drinking in the strong air with delight. "Isn't it glorious, Tommy?"

"Yes," said Tommy, doubtfully. He was pale, and presently he lay down in the bottom of the boat.

"Suck a lemon," suggested Judy, practically, "there are some in that little locker," and after following her advice, Tommy recovered sufficiently to sit up, and in the lulls of the gale he and Judy shrieked at each other, and sang songs of the sea.

They ate a little lunch, intermittently - a bite of sandwich while Tommy pulled at the ropes or adjusted the sail, or a wing of chicken as Judy swung the boat with her head to the wind. It was all very exciting and Judy forgot care and the worried hearts that she had left behind, and Tommy, reckless in a new-found courage, felt that he was a true sailor and a son of the sea.

But as the night wore on, and the wind settled into a steady blow, it took all Judy's science and Tommy's strength to keep the little boat in her course. The waves ran higher and higher, and Judy grew quiet, and her face was pale with fatigue.

Tommy began to have doubts. A life on the ocean wave wasn't all that it was cracked up to be, and anyhow, Judy was only a girl!

"How long before we get there," he shouted amid the tumult.

"We ought to reach the Point in a little while," said Judy, "but - but I am not quite sure where we are, Tommy. I have always kept within sight of land before -"

There was no land to be seen now. The moon was hidden by the clouds, and on each side of them black water stretched out to meet black sky, broken only by leaping lengths of white foam.

But they were not fated to reach the Point that night, for the wind changed, and in spite of all efforts to keep on their way, the little boat was blown farther and farther out into the great, wide waters of the bay.

"Is there any danger?" questioned Tommy as the foam boiled

up on each side of the boat, drenching both himself and Judy, whose face, white as a pearl, showed through the gloom.

But Judy did not answer at once. She waited until she could make herself heard in a lull of the wind, and then she admitted, "We shall have to stay out all night, I am afraid."

"All night," gasped Tommy. "Oh, Judy, ain't it awful."

"No," said Judy, calmly, "not if we are not silly and afraid."

"Oh, I'm not afraid," swaggered Tommy, "only I wish we hadn't come," he ended, weakly, as the boat swooped down into the trough of a wave, and then rose high in the air.

"You should have told me it wasn't safe," he complained presently, "you knew it was going to storm, didn't you?"

"Well, I like that -" Judy stared at him. "Oh, try to be a man, Tommy, if you are a coward."

Tommy winced. "I'm not afraid," he defended.

"Perhaps not," said Judy, slowly, "but - but - if you had been a man you would have said, 'I am sorry I asked you to bring me, Judy.'"

"But -"

"Oh, we won't argue." Judy raised her voice as another blast came. "I - I'm too tired to - to argue - Tommy -"

She swayed back and forth, holding on to the tiller weakly.

"I - I am so - tired," she tried to laugh, but her face was ghastly. "I - I guess I wasn't very nice just now, Tommy, - but I - am - so tired. You will have to steer, Tommy."

"But I don't know how," blubbered Tommy.

"You will just have to do it. I can't sit up -" and Judy tumbled down into the bottom of the boat, completely worn out from the unaccustomed strain.

Tommy whimpered in a frightened monotone as he grasped the tiller with inexperienced hands. What if Judy were dead? What - ? "I'll never do it again. I'll never run awa -" but Judy did not hear, for she lay with her eyes shut in a sort of stupor in the bottom of the boat.

She was waked by a bump and the wash of the waves over the boat.

"We've struck somewhere, Tommy," she shrieked.

"Oh, oh," howled Tommy, "we'll drown, Judy!"

"We won't," she said, tensely. "Hush, Tommy. *Hush* - do you hear? Can you swim?"

"No," and he clutched hold of her as another wave broke over the boat.

"There's a life-belt here somewhere," and Andy threw things out in frantic haste. "Here. Take hold of it, Tommy."

"But - what are you going to do?"

"I can swim. Don't mind about me, and if you keep quiet I will tow you in if we are near land."

She said it quietly, but in her heart she wondered where she would tow him.

"Don't take hold of me," she insisted, peremptorily, as she felt Tommy grab her arm, "or we shall both go under - oh -"

In that moment the boat keeled over, and when Judy came to the top of the water, she knew that between her and death in the green depths beneath, there was nothing but the strength of her frail limbs.

"Tommy," she called, as soon as she could get the salt water out of her mouth.

"Here," came shiveringly over the face of the waters.

"Are you all right?"

"No, no, it's horrid. Oh, I wish I was home - I wish I was home" - wailed Tommy, clinging to the belt for dear life.

The clouds had parted and one little star showed in the blackness, in the dim light Judy could just see Tommy's eyes glowing from out of his pallid face.

"He is afraid," she thought to herself, curiously. She was not afraid. She had never been afraid of the water - poor Tommy.

She felt strangely weak, however, and all at once there came to her the knowledge that she could not keep up any longer. The strength of the old days was not hers - and she was tired - so tired -

She caught hold of the life-belt, and as she did so Tommy screamed, "Don't, Judy. It won't hold us both. Don't -"

"He is afraid," she thought again, pityingly, "and I am not, and we can't both hold on to that belt -"

Tommy babbled crazily, bemoaning his danger, sobbing now and then - but Judy was very still.

"I can't keep up much longer. I mustn't try to hold on with Tommy. He is afraid - poor Tommy -" she looked up at the little star, "and I'm not afraid - I love the sea," she thought, dreamily. Then for one moment she came out of her trance.

"Tommy, Tommy!" she cried sharply.

"What?"

"Don't let go of the belt. Hold on, no matter how tired you are. In the morning - some one - will save you -"

"But you - wh-wh-at are you going to do, Judy?"

"Oh, I - ?" she laughed faintly. "Oh, I shall be all right - all right, Tommy," and her voice died away in an awful silence.

CHAPTER XXII

THE CASTAWAYS

"Judy -" shrieked Tommy, and suddenly the answer came in a choking cry of joy.

"I can touch bottom, Tommy, I thought I was sinking, but it isn't over our heads at all. We must be near shore."

Tommy put his feet down gingerly. He had hated to think of the untold fathoms beneath him - depths which in his imagination were strewn with shipwrecks and the bones of lost mariners.

So when his feet came in contact with good firm sand, he giggled hysterically.

"Gee, but it feels good," he said. "Are you all right, Judy?"

But Judy had waded in and dropped exhausted on the beach.

"I don't know," she said, feebly, "I guess so."

"Where are we?" asked Tommy, splashing his way to her side.

He surveyed the land around them. In the moonlight it showed nothing but wide beach and back of that stiff rustling sea-grass and mounds of sand like the graves of sailors dead and gone. Not a house was in sight - not a sign of life.

Temple Bailey

"I don't know where we are," Judy raised her head for a second, then dropped it back, "but we are safe, Tommy Tolliver, and that's something to be thankful for.

"I knew the sea wouldn't hurt me," she went on - a little wildly, perhaps, which was excusable after the danger she had escaped. "I knew it wouldn't hurt me."

"Oh, the sea," whined Tommy, disgustedly, "this isn't the ocean, and if just an old bay can act like this, why, I say give me land. No more water for me, thank you. I am going home and plow - yes, I am, I am going to plow, Judy Jameson, and take care of the cows - and - and weed the garden," naming the thing he hated most as a climax, "and when I get to thinking things are hard, I will remember this night - when I was a shipwrecked mariner."

In imagination he was revelling in the story he would tell at home. Of the adventures that he would relate to the eager ears of the youth of Fairfax. "Yes, indeed, I will remember the time when I was a shipwrecked mariner," he said with gusto, "and lived on a desert island."

"Oh, Tommy," in spite of faintness and hunger and exhaustion, Judy laughed. "Oh, Tommy, you funny boy - this isn't a desert island."

"How do you know it isn't?" asked Tommy, stubbornly.

"There aren't any desert islands in the bay."

"I'll bet this is one."

"I hope not."

"Why?"

"We haven't anything to eat."

"Oh, well, we will find things in the morning."

"Where?"

"On the trees. Fruit and things."

"But there aren't any trees."

"Oh, well, oysters then."

"How will you get them -"

"And fish," ignoring difficulties.

"We haven't any lines or hooks."

"And things from the wreck."

"The boat tipped over," said Judy, with a little sobbing sigh for the capsized "Princess," "and anyhow there was nothing left to eat but some lemons and a box of crackers."

"Don't be so discouraging," grumbled Tommy, "you know people always find something."

They sat in silence for a time, and then Judy said:

"I hope they are not worrying at home."

"Gee - they will be scared, when they wake up in the morning and find you gone," said Tommy, consolingly.

"I left a note for Anne in the library, telling her where I had gone - but I thought I would get back before she found it," said Judy - "poor little Anne."

"I think it is poor Tommy and poor Judy," said the cause of all the trouble.

"But we deserve it and Anne doesn't. And that's the diffe-rence," said Judy, wisely.

"Aw - don't preach."

"Couldn't if I tried," and Judy clasped her hands around her knees and gazed out on the dark waters, and again there was a long silence.

"Well, what are we going to do?" demanded Tommy as the night wind blew cold against his wet garments and made him shiver.

"Do?"

"Yes. We can't sit like this all night."

"Guess we shall have to."

Another silence.

"Gee, I'm hungry."

"So am I."

"But there isn't anything to eat."

"No."

Silence again.

"Gee - I'm sleepy."

"Find some place out of the wind and go to sleep. I'll watch."

"All night?"

"Perhaps. You go to sleep, Tommy."

"Won't you be lonesome?"

Judy smiled wearily. "No," she said, "you go to sleep, Tommy."

And Tommy went.

But it was not until the cold light of dawn touched the face of the waters, that the sentinel-like figure on the beach relaxed from its strained position, and then the dark head dropped, and with a sigh Judy stretched her slender body on the hard sand, and she, too, slept.

CHAPTER XXIII

IN A SILVER BOAT

The tide coming in the next morning brought with it on the blue surface of the waves two bobbing lemons. Many times the golden globes rolled up the beach only to be carried back by the under-wash of the waters, but finally one wave rolling farther than the rest left them high and dry on the sand, and the same wave splashing over an inert and huddled up figure waked it to consciousness.

Judy sat up stiffly and stared around her. "Oh," she sighed, as she remembered all that had happened in the darkness of the night.

She clasped her hands around her knees and gazed out forlornly over the empty waters. Not a sail, not a trail of smoke broke the blueness of the bay. With another sigh, this time of disappointment, she turned her gaze landward, and beheld there nothing but lank marsh grass and sand and driftwood.

And then at her feet she spied the lemons. She picked them up - they were the only salvage from the sunken boat. She looked around for Tommy. On the other side of a mound of sand, she could just see the top of his head, and as he did not move she decided that he was still asleep.

Her eyes twinkled, as with stealthy steps she crept up the beach until she reached a low bush with scrubby sage-green foliage.

On its spiky branches she stuck the lemons, and then ran swiftly back.

Tommy was still sleeping, so she dipped her hands into the cold water, took off her stiffened shoes and bathed her swollen feet. Her dress had dried in the night winds, and when she had combed her hair she looked fairly presentable.

Barefooted she tripped over the cool wet sands, glorying in the broad expanse of blue, with white gulls dipping to it from a bluer sky.

"Tommy," she called, "Tommy."

A towsled head appeared over the top of the mound.

"Oh, dear," said Tommy, lugubriously, as he saw her sparkling face, "you act as if being shipwrecked was a good joke, Judy."

"The sun is shining and it is perfectly fine."

"It's perfectly horrid," said Tommy.

Judy looked at him for a moment, and a lump came in her throat.

"Well, it seems so much better to laugh over our troubles than to cry. Don't you think so, Tommy?" she said, wistfully, and tears welled up into her brave eyes.

"Oh, don't cry, Judy," begged Tommy, who felt that all the world would grow dark if Judy's staunch heart should fail. "Don't cry, Judy." She brushed away her tears and smiled at him. "Well, get up, lazy boy," she said.

"I'm hungry."

"Well, go and hunt for something to eat."

"Don't know where to look."

"Neither did Robinson Crusoe."

"Oh, well, what are you going to do?"

"Watch for some one to come and take us off."

It began to be exciting. If Tommy had not been so hungry, he really believed that he might have appreciated the adventure. But his soul yearned for hot cakes and maple syrup, or beefsteak and waffles - or at least for plain bread and butter.

"Gee, but it would taste good," he said aloud.

"What?"

"I was thinking of breakfast," said poor Tommy, "hot rolls and things like that, Judy."

"O-o-oh," said Judy, "how about some hot biscuit, with one of Perkins' omelettes - and - creamed potatoes?"

"Oh, don't," groaned hungry Tommy, and fled.

He came back in about two minutes, swaggering with importance.

"This island isn't so barren as it looks," he said, pompously. "You don't know everything, Judy."

"Don't I?"

"No. Now what do you think of these," and he produced the two lemons triumphantly.

"Where did you find them?"

"Growing over there," and he pointed to the scrubby,

sage-green spiky bush.

"Who would have believed it?" Judy's eyes were round and solemn, but the expression in them should have warned Tommy.

"You see there are some things you don't know. I'm going to look for oysters now."

"Oysters -"

"Yes. To eat with our lemons."

"You might find some cracker fruit, and a coffee vine, and maybe there will be a salt and pepper tree somewhere - and Tommy, *please* discover a Tabasco bush - I never could eat my oysters without Tabasco."

Tommy looked at her wrathfully. "Aw, Judy," he said, with a red face, "you're foolin' - and I think it's mean."

Then a thought struck him, and he examined the lemons carefully.

"You stuck them on that bush," he accused, excitedly. "There are holes in them. You did it to fool me, didn't you, Judy?"

She nodded.

"An' you think it's a joke - I - I -" He could think of nothing sufficiently crushing to say. "Well, I don't," he finished sulkily, and plumped himself down on the sand, with his face away from her.

"Tommy," she said, after a long silence, "Tommy."

"Huh?"

"Please be good-natured."

"Be good-natured yourself," said Tommy, with a half-sob. "I'm - I'm - perfectly mis'able, Judy Jameson -"

It was then that Judy showed that she could be womanly and sympathetic. "I'm sorry I teased you, Tommy," she said, softly. "Let's make ourselves comfortable here on the sand, and I'll tell you about when I used to live in Europe."

Tommy liked that, and all the morning Judy talked, although she was so tired, that her head felt light, and her eyes blurred, but Tommy was happy and she tried to forget about herself.

She made him suck both of the lemons.

"I don't want any," she said, although her throat was so dry that she could hardly speak. "I don't want any."

"Whew, but they are sour," said Tommy, and made a wry face, but he did not insist upon her having one.

That was the worst of it, the thirst, for there was no fresh water.

"Let's explore," said Tommy, as the afternoon waned and no relief came. "Maybe we will find a house back there somewhere."

But Judy shook her head. "No," she said, "we are on the end of the peninsula, between the bay and the ocean. It is just salt marshes from one end to the other, and no one lives on them. The best thing we can do is to hail a boat."

"But there ain't any boats."

"There will be," said Judy, stoutly. "There are lots of little schooners that take fruit and vegetables to the markets. Not many of them come this way, but some of them do, and if we wait they will rescue us."

After that they saw several sails, and waved Tommy's coat frantically, but no one responded. As the twilight darkened into the night, a steamer went by, her lights shining like jewels against the purple background - red and green and yellow.

"If we only had a lantern," groaned Judy, as Tommy shouted himself hoarse, and the steamer kept on her majestic way, leaving them hopelessly behind.

"Maybe some one will see us in the morning." Judy was trying to encourage Tommy, who had dropped down on the sand with his back to her, but not before she had seen his working face, and his knuckles rubbing his red eyes.

"I'm going to sleep," he muttered, still with his face away from her, and with that he curled himself up against the big mound, as he had done the night before, and forgot his troubles.

Judy lay on the sand watching the waves roll in, and thinking long thoughts. She thought of her father, living, perhaps, on some such lonely beach as this, but farther away from the haunts of men - alone, looking at the same stars, searching a vaster expanse for the ship that never came. She thought, too, of her mother, the gentle mother, whose guarding presence she seemed to feel in the wonderful stillness. She thought of their plans for her; that she might grow to gracious womanhood, following in the footsteps of the women of her race, and here she was - a runaway, reckless little girl, away from home at midnight, chaperoned only by the wind and the waves, and with no roof above her but the sky!

Under the solemn canopy of the night she made many resolves, cried a little, and lay there with her eyes shut, but not asleep, feeling very wicked, and very forlorn, and very, very hopeless.

When she opened her eyes again, the night was glorious. The moon had risen, and its light made a silver pathway across the darkness of the waters, and sailing straight towards her, its sails set to the fair winds of heaven, came a little boat, dark against the shining background.

Some one stood in the bow, straight and strong and young, and as Judy watched in a half-dream, she remembered an opera she had seen once upon a time; where a knight in silver armor had come on the back of a silver swan to the lady he loved. She had hoped, mistily, that when she was old enough for such things, that Love might come to her like that - over the sea in silver armor, and sail away with her in a silver boat to the end of the world!

The boat came nearer, the boat with the silver sails! She stood up to watch, and as her slim figure was etched sharply against the background of white sand, there came to her upon the wings of the night the cry -

"Judy!"

Her hand went to her heart. Was it real? Where did he come from, that youth in the silver boat. But even as she wondered, the cry went back to him, an answering cry, joyous, welcoming

"Launcelot, oh, Launcelot."

CHAPTER XXIV

"HOME IS THE SAILOR FROM THE SEA"

Judy's cry did not wake Tommy, and still in a half-dream she went down to the edge of the water and stood ghost-like in the moonlight, waiting. There was another figure in the boat, half-hidden by the shadowy sails, but it was Launcelot who, when the shallow water was reached, jumped out and waded to shore.

"Judy, Judy," he said, as he came up to her, "I knew I should find you."

She looked at him with wide eyes. "Where - where did you come from," she whispered, while her white hands fluttered across his coat sleeve as if to see that he was real.

There was sympathy and tenderness in his boyish face, but seeing her condition, he spoke cheerfully. "I came down to The Breakers after Tommy. His mother was ill, and his father had to stay with her, so they sent me. And when I got there I found Anne and - and -" he checked himself hurriedly, "I found Anne almost frantic because you had gone, and then when she found your note I started out, for I knew I should find you, Judy. I knew I should sail straight to you."

For one little moment as they stood together in the moonlight, he looked down at her with the eyes of the lover he was to be, but as yet they were only boy and girl and the moment passed.

Temple Bailey

"Where's Tommy?" asked Launcelot, coming out of his dream.

He was answered by a shout as Tommy came plunging over the sand.

"Why didn't you wake me, Judy?" he complained, bitterly, "when you first saw the boat."

"Stop that," commanded Launcelot. "Why weren't you keeping watch? What kind of sailor do you call yourself, Tommy?"

"Oh, well," Tommy excused, "I was sleepy."

"And so you let a girl watch," was Launcelot's hard way of putting it, and Tommy's eyes shifted.

"Oh, well," he began again.

"I made him let me watch, Launcelot," Judy interrupted, feeling sorry for the small boy, "and I told him to go to sleep."

"Oh, of course you did," said Launcelot, shortly, "and of course he went, he's a nice sort of sailor."

"I'm not going to be a sailor," Tommy announced, sulkily. "I'm going home -"

"Right-o," agreed Lancelot, "and the quicker the better."

"Miss Judy," came a sepulchral voice from the boat, "Miss Judy, we thought you were drownded."

"Oh, Perkins," cried Judy, "is that you, Perkins?"

"What's left of me, Miss," and Perkins' bald head came into view as he stood up in the boat.

Judy and Tommy climbed in, amid excited questions and

explanations, which presently settled into a continuous monotone of complaint from Tommy. "I'm half-starved. Haven't you anything to eat, Perkins?"

Now Tommy grated on Perkins' nerves. The old butler had always been treated by the Jamesons with the gentle consideration due his age and long and faithful service, in the light of which Tommy's dictation seemed nothing less than impertinent.

And so it came about that Judy was served with good things first, while Tommy was made to wait.

"Oh, Perkins, can't you hurry," growled the small rude boy.

And then Judy turned on him. "You may be hungry, Tommy," she blazed, "but don't speak to Perkins that way again."

"Oh, Miss," deprecated Perkins, although in his old heart he was glad of her defense.

"Perkins has been out all night hunting for us," Judy's voice quivered, "and - and - he is just as tired as we are, Tommy Tolliver."

But Tommy had his sandwich, and blissfully munching it, cared little for Judy's reproof. After he had finished he went to sleep comfortably in the bottom of the boat, his troubles forgotten.

There was about Launcelot and Perkins an air of subdued excitement that finally attracted Judy's attention.

"What's the matter with you all?" she asked, curiously, as she looked up suddenly from her pile of comfortable cushions, and caught Perkins smiling at Launcelot over her head.

"Oh, nothing, Miss, nothing at all," coughed Perkins.

"Has anything happened?"

Launcelot, who was steering, smiled down at her.

"Miss Curiosity," he teased.

"I'm not curious. I just want to know."

"Oh, well, that's one way to put it."

"Tell me. Has anything happened?"

"Yes."

"What?"

"Something splendid."

Judy sat up. "Tell me," she begged.

But Launcelot was inflexible. "Not now," and Judy sank back with a sigh, for she was getting to know that when the big boy said a thing he meant it.

"When will I know?" she asked after a while.

"When you get to The Breakers."

"Oh."

She was silent for a little, then she said:

"I know you think it was awful for me to run away with Tommy -"

"It would have been better if you had sent him home."

"But I wanted to help him - he has such a hard time."

"He would have a harder time if he went to sea, Judy. He isn't like you, he doesn't like the sea for its own sake. He has read a lot of stuff about sailors and adventures, and his head is full of it. He isn't the kind that makes a brave man."

"I know that," said Judy, for the little voyage had proved Tommy and had found him wanting.

"He ought to stay at home and fight things out," said Launcelot, "as the rest of us have to."

Judy looked up at him, surprised. "Are you fighting things out?" she asked.

"Oh, yes. I want to go to college, and I can't and that's the end of it," and Launcelot's lips were set in a stern line.

"Why not?"

"Father's too sick for me to leave - I've got to run the farm," was Launcelot's simple statement of the bitter fact.

"I am always trying to do great things," mourned Judy, with a sigh for the Cause of Thomas the Downtrodden, from which the romance seemed to have fled, "but they just fizzle out."

"Don't be discouraged. You'll learn to look before you leap yet, Judy," and Launcelot laughed, his own troubles forgotten in his interest in hers.

"What are you going to take up for a life work?" asked Judy, remembering Ruskin.

"I am going to be a lawyer," announced Launcelot, promptly, "and a good one like the Judge. My grandfather was a Judge, too, but father chose business, and failed because he wasn't fitted for it, and that's why we are on the farm, now."

"I'm going to be an artist," announced Judy, toploftically,

"and paint wonderful pictures."

But Launcelot looked at her doubtfully. "I'll bet you won't," he said with decision. "I'll bet you won't paint pictures and be an artist."

"Why not?"

"Because you'll get married, and -"

Judy shrugged an impatient shoulder. "I am never going to marry," she declared.

"Why not?"

"Because I want my own way," said wilful Judy.

"Oh," said "bossy" Launcelot.

The waves were twinkling in the gold of the morning sun when the tired party sighted the beach below The Breakers.

Judy standing up in the boat with her dark hair blowing around her spied a little waiting group.

"There's Anne - dear Anne - and, why, Launcelot, there's a dog."

"Is there?"

"Yes, and - and - a man -"

"Yes." Launcelot's voice was calm, but his hand on the tiller trembled.

She turned on him her startled eyes. "Do you know who it is?" she demanded.

"Yes."

"Who?"

"Look and see."

The man on the beach was gazing straight out across the bay, and in the clearness of the morning air, Judy made out his features, the pale dark face, the waving hair.

She clutched Launcelot's arm. "Who is it?" she demanded, looking as if she had seen a spirit. "Who is it, Launcelot?"

And then Launcelot gave a shout that woke Tommy.

"It's, oh, *who* do you think it is, Judy Jameson?"

And Judy whispered with a white face, "It looks like - my father. Is it really - my father - Launcelot?" and Launcelot let the tiller go, and caught hold of her hands, and said: "It really is, it really and truly is, Judy Jameson."

Judy never knew how the boat reached the wharf, nor how she came to be in her father's arms. But she knew that she should never be happier this side of heaven than she was when he held her close and murmured in her ear, "My own daughter, my own dear little girl."

It was an excited group that circled around them - Perkins and Launcelot, and the dog, Terry, and last but not least, Anne, red-eyed and dishevelled.

"Oh, Judy, Judy," she sobbed, when at last Judy came down to earth and beamed on her. "We thought you were drowned, and I have cried all night."

And at that Judy cried, too, and they sat down on the sand and had a little weep together, comfortably, as girls will, when the danger is over and every one is safe and happy.

"I'm all right," gasped Judy at last, mopping her eyes with a clean handkerchief, offered her by the ever-useful Perkins. "I'm all right - but - but - Anne was such a goosie, - and I am so happy -" And with that she dropped her head on Anne's shoulder again and cried harder than ever.

"Dear heart, don't cry," begged the Captain.

"She is tired to death," explained Launcelot.

"She needs her breakfast, sir," suggested Perkins.

"So do I," grumbled Tommy Tolliver, who stood in the background feeling very much left out.

But even as they spoke, Judy slipped into her father's arms again, and lay there quietly, as she murmured, so that no one else heard:

"'Home is the sailor from the sea' - oh, father, father, I knew you would come back to me - I knew you would come back some day."

CHAPTER XXV

LAUNCELOT BUYS A COW

Never had Fairfax seen so many interesting arrivals as during that second week in August.

On Monday came Dr. Grennell, mysterious and smiling; on Tuesday, Judge Jameson, pale but radiant; on Wednesday, Tommy and Launcelot, bursting with important news; on Thursday, Captain Jameson, with a joyful dark maiden on one side of him, and a joyful fair maiden on the other; on Friday, Perkins, beaming with the baggage, and on Saturday, the Terry-dog, resignedly, in a crate.

And every one, except Terry, the dog, had a story to tell, and the story was one that was to become a classic in the annals of Fairfax. How Captain Jameson had been washed overboard in southern seas, how he had been rescued by natives and had lived among them; how he had been found by a party searching for gold; how he had started with them for home, had become ill as soon as they put to sea, and because of his illness had been the only one left when the ship caught on fire; how the fire had gone out, and he had floated on the deserted vessel until picked up by a fishing-boat, and how he had been brought to Newfoundland and how Dr. Grennell had discovered him by means of the Spanish coins.

But in the eyes of the children of Fairfax his adventures paled before those of Tommy Tolliver. To a gaping audience that small boy talked of the things he had done - of shipwrecks, of desert islands, of hunger and thirst until the little girls gazed at him with tears in their eyes, although the effect was somewhat spoiled by Jimmie Jones' artless remark, "But you were only away four days, Tommy!"

All Fairfax rejoiced with the Judge and Judy, but only little Anne knew what Judy really felt, for in the first moment that they were alone together after that eventful morning at The Breakers, Judy, with her eyes shining like stars, had thrown her arms around the neck of her fair little friend, and had whispered, "Oh, Anne, *Anne*, I don't deserve such happiness, but I am so thankful that I feel as if I should be good for the rest of my life."

And no one but Anne knew why Judy put everything aside to be with her father, to anticipate every desire of his, to cheer every solitary minute.

"I must try to take mother's place," she confided to her sympathetic listener in the watches of the night. "He misses her so - Anne."

Anne went back to the little gray house, where the plums were purple on the tree in the orchard, and where Becky on her lookout limb was hidden by the thickness of the foliage. The robins were gone, and so was Belinda's occupation, but she had more important things on hand, and after the first joy of greetings, the little grandmother led Anne to a cozy corner of the little kitchen, where in a big basket, Belinda sang lullabies to four happy, sleepy balls of down as white as herself.

"Oh, the dear little pussy cats," gurgled Anne, as Belinda welcomed her with a gratified "Purr-up," "what does Becky think of them, grandmother?"

"She takes care of them when Belinda goes out," said the little grandmother. "It's too funny to see them cuddle under her black wings."

"I wonder if she will make friends with Terry, Judy's dog," chatted Anne, as she cuddled the precious kittens. "He's the dearest thing, and he took to Judy right away, and follows her around all the time."

The little grandmother sat down in an old rocker with a red cushion and took off her spectacles with trembling hands. "Belinda will have to get used to him, I guess," she said.

"Of course," said Anne, not looking up, "Judy will bring him here when she comes."

"I don't mean that," said the little grandmother.

Something in the old voice made Anne look up.

"What's the matter, little grandmother?" she asked, anxiously.

"I mean that we are going to leave the little gray house, Anne, you and I and Belinda and Becky," and with that the little grandmother put on her spectacles again, to see how Anne took the news.

Anne stared. "Leave the little gray house," she said, slowly. "Why what do you mean, grandmother?"

"We are going to live at the Judge's," and at that Anne's face changed from dismay to happiness, and she turned the kittens over to Belinda and flung her arms around the little old lady's neck.

"Oh, am I really going to live with Judy?" she shrieked joyfully, "and you and Becky and Belinda - oh, it's too good to be true."

"We really are," said Mrs. Batcheller. "The Judge and I had a long talk together, the day he came down, and he wants you to go away to school with Judy, and have me come and help Aunt Patterson to manage his house. He says she is too feeble for so much care and that it will be an accommodation to him."

But Mrs. Batcheller did not tell how the Judge had argued for hours to break down the barriers of pride which she had raised, and that he had finally won, because of his insistence that Anne must have the opportunities due one of her name and race.

"You are to go to Mrs. French's school in Richmond, with Judy. She is a gentlewoman, a Southerner, and an old friend of the Judge's and mine, and we think it will be exactly the place for you two for a time."

"It will be lovely," cried little Anne, as the plans for her future were unfolded, but late that evening when she was ready to say "good night" she stood for a moment with her cheek against her grandmother's soft old one.

"I shall miss you and the little gray house, grandmother," she whispered, "I was hungry for you at The Breakers, although it was lovely there, and every one was so kind."

"I shall miss you too, dear heart," said the little grandmother, but she did not say how much, for she wanted Anne to go away happily, and she felt that she must not be selfish.

It was wonderful the planning that went on after that. Anne spent many days at the big house in Fairfax, and each time she went it was a tenderer, dearer Judy that welcomed her.

"Father will stay with grandfather this winter. I begged to stay, too, but they both think the schools here are not what I need, and so I am to go away," she explained one morning as she and Anne were getting ready to go with a party of young people to pick goldenrod.

"Yes," said Anne, putting her red reefer over her white dress, and admiring the effect.

"I hate school," began Judy, sticking in a hat-pin viciously, then she stopped and laughed, "No, I don't, either. I don't hate anything since father came back."

"Not even cats?" asked Anne, demurely.

"No. You know I love Belinda."

"Nor picnics?"

"Not Fairfax ones."

"Nor books?"

"I just love 'em - thanks to you."

"Nor - nor boys -?" mischievously.

"Oh, do stop your questions," and Judy put her hands over her ears. But Anne persisted, "Nor boys, Judy?"

"I like Launcelot Bart - and - little Jimmie Jones, but I am not sure about Tommy Tolliver, Anne."

And then they both laughed light-heartedly, and tripped down-stairs to find Amelia and Nannie and Tommy waiting for them.

"Launcelot couldn't come," explained Tommy. "He had to go to Upper Fairfax, and he said he was awfully sorry, but he didn't dare to take so much time away from the farm."

"Poor fellow," sighed tender-hearted little Anne. "He is always so busy."

"I don't think he is to be pitied," said Judy, with a scornful glance at Tommy. "He has work to do and he does it, which is more than most people do."

There was gold in the sunshine, and gold in the changing leaves, and gold in the ripened grain in the fields, and gold in the goldenrod which they had come to pick.

Tommy gathered great armfuls of the feathery bloom, and the girls made it into bunches, while Terry, who had come with them, whuffed at the chipmunks on the gray fence-rails.

"What do you want it for?" asked Tommy, sitting down beside the busy maidens and wiping his warm forehead.

"To-morrow is Judy's birthday," said Anne, "and we are going to decorate the house."

"Oh, is it?" asked Amelia and Nannie together.

"Yes," said Judy, "and I want you to come to dinner and spend the evening with us. I am not going to have a party, because father isn't feeling as if he wanted to join in any gay things yet, but we can have a nice time together, and it may be the last before Anne and I go away to school."

"*Go where?*" gasped Nannie and Amelia and Tommy.

Judy explained. "We leave the first week in September," she ended.

"Oh, oh," cried the stricken three, "what shall we do. All winter - and we can't have any fun - if Anne isn't here, nor you, Judy, and we had planned so many things."

"Will you really miss *me*?" Judy asked a little wistfully, and at that Nannie's hand was laid on hers, as the little girl murmured, "We shall miss you awfly, Judy," while Amelia sighed a great, gusty sigh, as she said, "Oh, dear, now everything's spoiled!"

"Do you want me to come to your birthday dinner, too?" asked Tommy, anxiously, when the first shock of the coming separation was over, "or ain't you goin' to have any boys."

"Yes, I want you and Launcelot," said Judy, who had debated the question of being friendly with Tommy, for he hadn't seemed worth it, but Anne had pleaded for him. "He really means well, Judy," she had protested, "and I think he is going to turn over a new leaf."

"Well, I hope he will," said Judy, and forgave him.

When the big gate was reached, Nannie and Amelia and Tommy went on, and as Judy and Anne went into the old garden, they found the Judge and the Captain, both still semi-invalids, sitting there, amid a riot of late summer blossoms.

As he greeted them, Captain Jameson's eyes went from the rosy, fair face of little Anne to the pale but happy one of his daughter. "Father is right," he thought, "Anne does her good."

"Isn't it lovely here," said Judy, dropping her great golden bunch with a sigh as she sat down on the bench under the lilac bush. "It's so cool."

"What a lot of goldenrod," said the Judge. "Aren't you tired?"

"A little," said Judy, as she took off her hat.

"Launcelot couldn't go," Anne started to explain, when Terry, who had been investigating the hedge, barked.

"What's the matter with him?" asked Judy, as the small dog growled in what might be called a perfunctory fashion, for he was so good natured that he was in a chronic state of being at peace with the world.

She went to the gate and looked over.

"Why, it's a cow," she cried, "a beautiful little brown-eyed cow."

Terry barked again, and then a voice outside the hedge said: "Yes, and I've just bought her."

"Launcelot," screamed both of the girls, delightedly, and opened the gate wide.

CHAPTER XXVI

JUDY PLAYS LADY BOUNTIFUL

"Down, Terry," commanded the Captain, as the little dog went for the mild-eyed cow, but the mild-eyed cow seemed perfectly able to take care of herself, and as she lowered her horns, Terry retired discreetly to a safe place between the Captain's knees, where he wagged an ingratiating tail.

Launcelot and the cow stood framed in the rose-covered gateway.

"Yes, I've bought a cow," explained the big boy, who was dusty but cheerful, "and we are going to have our own butter and milk, and if there is any over, I'll sell it."

"You have my order now," said the Judge, handsomely.

"Thank you, sir," said Launcelot, and Anne cried:

"Oh, Launcelot, make it in little pats stamped with a violet, and label it, 'From the Violet Farm.'"

"That's not a bad idea," commended the Captain, "novelties like that take, and if the butter is good, you may get a market for more than you can make."

"Then I will get another cow and enlarge my hothouse, and between the butter and the violets I guess I can bring up my college fund," and Launcelot looked so hopeful that they all smiled in sympathy.

"Where did you get her?" asked Judy, as she patted the pretty creature on the head.

"I bought her a mile or so out in the country, and I tell you I hated to take her after I had paid the money."

"Why?" asked Anne.

"Oh, they were so poor, and the cow was the only thing they had. There is a widow, named McSwiggins, with six children, and I guess they have had a pretty hard time, and now their taxes are due and the interest and two of them have had the typhoid fever, and are just skin and bone, and they had to sell the cow, and they cried, and I felt like a thief when I carried her off."

"Oh, poor things," cried Judy, when Launcelot finished his breathless recital, "poor things."

"I didn't want to take her, after I found out, but Mrs. McSwiggins said that they needed the money awfully, and that I was doing them a favor - only it was hard, and then she cried and the children all cried, too."

"Why haven't they told some one before this?" asked the Judge, wiping his eyes.

"I guess the mother is too proud. They are from the South and they haven't been in this neighborhood long, and she don't know any one."

"What's the cow's name?" asked Anne, whose eyes were like dewy forget-me-nots.

"Sweetheart. The biggest girl named her, and when I went out of the gate she just sat down on the step and looked after us, and her eyes hurt me, they were so sad."

The little cow moved restlessly. "I guess I'll have to go," sighed Launcelot, standing like a Peri outside the gates of Paradise, and contrasting the coolness and quiet of the old garden with the heat and dust of the long white road. "I guess I'll have to take Sweetheart on."

But just then down the path came Perkins, dignified in white linen, and in his hand he bore a tray on which a glass pitcher, misty with coolness and showing ravishing glimpses of lemon peel and ice, promised delicious refreshment.

"You come and have some lemonade, Mr. Launcelot," said Perkins, as he set the tray on the table, "I'll hold the cow."

And, as they all insisted, Launcelot came in, and Perkins went without the gate.

But, alas, Sweetheart was a cow of many moods, and as the gay little party in the garden sipped the cooling drink in the shade of the trees, the little cow, growing restive out there in the sun with the flies worrying her, suddenly ducked her head and ran.

And after her, still holding the rope, went the immaculate Perkins, to be dragged hither and thither by her erratic movements, while he shouted desperately, "Whoa."

And after Perkins went the excited Terry-dog, and after Terry went Launcelot, and after Launcelot went Judy, and then Anne, and then far in the rear, the Judge, while Captain Jameson, too weak to run, stood at the gate and watched.

It was a brave race. Perkins had grit and he would not let go of the rope, and Sweetheart wanted to go home and she would not stop running, and so the procession went up the dusty road and down a dusty hill, and then up another dusty hill, and down a cool green bank, where seeing ahead of her a murmuring limpid stream, Sweetheart dashed into it, stood

Temple Bailey

still, and placidly drank in long sighing gulps.

Perkins went in after her, and was rescued by Launcelot, while Judy and Anne stood on the bank and laughed until the tears ran down their cheeks.

Perkins laughed, too, as he emerged wet and dripping, but beaming.

"I didn't let her go," he chuckled, a little proud of his agility in his old age, and Launcelot said admiringly, "I didn't think you had it in you, Perkins," and at that Perkins chuckled more than ever.

They went back in a triumphal procession, and then Lancelot took Sweetheart away with him, and the little girls went upstairs to dress.

The Captain and the Judge were left alone, and presently the former said:

"Why can't we put Launcelot through college, father? It's a shame he should have to work so hard."

But the Judge shook his head. "He is having something better than college, Philip," he said. "He is learning self-reliance and he will get to college if he keeps on like this and be better for the struggle. I've told Grennell a half-dozen times that I would put up the money, for I like the boy - but there is one very good reason why we can't pay his way."

"What's that?" asked the Captain, with interest.

"He won't take a cent from anybody," said the Judge, "and I like his independence."

"So do I," said the Captain, heartily, "but we will keep an eye on him, father, and help him out when we can."

An hour later as the Captain sat alone under the lilac bush, Judy came down with white ruffles a-flutter and with her brown locks beautifully combed and sat beside him.

"To-morrow is my birthday," she said, superfluously.

"My big girl," smiled the Captain, "you make me feel old, Judy mine."

She smiled back, abstractedly. "Are - are you going to give me a present, father?" she stammered.

It was a queer question, and the Captain was not sure that he liked it. Birthday presents were not to be talked about beforehand.

"Of course I am," he said, finally. "Why?"

"Will it - cost - as much as - Launcelot's cow?" asked Judy, still blushing.

"As Launcelot's cow?"

He stared at her. "Why do you want to know?" he asked.

"Well," she patted his coat collar, coaxingly, "I want you to give me the money, and let me buy back the McSwiggins cow.

"I'll buy it myself."

But she shook her head. "No, I want to give it myself. I feel - so - so - thankful, father, for my happiness, that I want to do something for somebody else, who isn't happy."

He put his hand under her chin and turned her face with its earnest eyes up to him. "You are sure you would rather have that than any other birthday present, Judy mine?" he asked, thinking how much she looked like her mother.

Temple Bailey

"I am very sure, father."

They sent for Launcelot that evening, and he entered into the plan with enthusiasm. "I can get another cow," he said, "and if they have the money and the cow both they will get along all right."

"I don't want them to know who gives it," said Judy. "I hate that way of giving. I don't want to go and stare at them and talk to them about their poverty. I think it would be nice to tie a note to Sweetheart's horns and just leave her there."

The next day about noon, a mysterious party, with a strange and unusual looking cow in their midst, crept to the back of the McSwiggins barn. Sweetheart lowed softly, as she recognized the familiar surroundings.

"Gracious, I hope they won't hear," said little Anne, "that would spoil it all."

Perkins set a heavy basket down and wiped his forehead.

"You go and look, Mr. Launcelot," he said, "and if there ain't any one around you tie her to the hitching-post, and then bring the ends of those pink ribbons back with you."

When that was accomplished, the Mysterious Four hid themselves in some bushes by the side of the road to await developments.

Presently Johnny McSwiggins, trailing listlessly towards the barn, gave one look and rushed back into the house.

"They's somethin' out thar," he said, with his eyes bulging.

Mary McSwiggins, the oldest girl, looked at him hopelessly. "I don' care ef they is. We alls too po' fer anythin' to hurt."

"But hit looks lak Sweetheart's ghos'," declared Johnny, "an' hit's got pink ribbin on. I declar' hit look lak Sweetheart's ghos', Sistuh Ma'y."

At that beloved name, Mary rushed out, while the family trailed behind, Mrs. McSwiggins bringing up the rear with the wan baby in her arms.

Tied to the post was Sweetheart, but such a cow had never been seen before in the history of Fairfax, for Judy was nothing if not original, and with the help of Anne and Launcelot she had decked the little cow gorgeously.

Around her neck was a huge wreath of roses, pink ribbons were tied to her horns, and two long pink streamers like reins went over her back and across the path and around the barn, where the ends were hidden.

"Gee," said Johnny McSwiggins, but the rest of them were silent, gazing at this transformed and glorified Sweetheart, while Mary laid her head against the sleek neck and murmured love names to her dear little cow.

"They's somethin' at the end of them ribbins," said Mrs. McSwiggins, after awhile, "you all go an' look."

And when they looked they found two huge baskets, one filled with wonderful things all ready to eat (Perkins had packed that), and the other filled with fruits and vegetables (Launcelot had raised them), and on top of one basket was a box of candy (Anne sat up to make it), and on the other a package of raisin cookies (from the little grandmother).

The little McSwiggins squealed and gurgled with delight, and then ate as only people can who have seen the gaunt wolf of starvation at the door, and as they ate they asked the question unceasingly:

"Who sent it?"

Temple Bailey

"They's a letter tied to her horn," volunteered Johnny McSwiggins after he had devoured two cookies and three sandwiches and a chicken leg. "I seen it."

They found it under the roses, and when they opened it, there dropped out two yellow-backed bills (from the Judge and the Captain), and a note (and that was from Judy), and the note said:

> "I waved my wand and commanded that Sweetheart be brought back to you. Also these other gifts. If you wish to keep them, and to keep my favor, you must never ask whence they came.
>
> "Your guardian fairy,
> "JUANNLOT."

Then all the little McSwiggins stared, and the littlest McSwiggins - except the baby, asked, "Was it really a fairy, mother?" and Mrs. McSwiggins wiped her eyes and sobbed, "I reckon it was, honey," but Mary McSwiggins with her eyes shining as they had never shone before in her sad little life said softly to her mother, "I'll bet it was them girls and that Bart boy. I'll bet it was -"

"What girls?" asked Mrs. McSwiggins.

"Them girls down at the Judge's in the big house. They wears white dresses, and one's got yaller hair and the other's got brown, and I was behin' the fence yustiddy when they was pickin' flowers, and that's how I foun' out they names - the dark one's Judy, and the light one's Anne - and the boy's named Launcelot. And that's how they got that fairy name - you look here," and she held up the note to her mother, "'Ju - ann - lot' - it's jes' them names strung together."

"Well, now," said Mrs. McSwiggins, "if that ain' bright, honey. But I don't know's we ought to take all them things."

"Sweetheart ain't goin' away from yer no more," said Mary, firmly, "and they'd feel mighty bad if we didn't take the other things."

"Well, mebbe they would," said Mrs. McSwiggins, "and anyhow they's saved us from the po'house, and that's a fact, Mary, and don' you forgit it when you say yo' prayers."

Far down the road the Mysterious Four gloated over their success.

"Wasn't it fun?" gasped Anne.

"Here's to the fairy Juannlot," cried Launcelot.

"May she never cease to do good," cried Judy, beaming on her fellow conspirators.

But Perkins merely nodded approval. For had not all the good ladies of the house of Jameson played the role of Lady Bountiful, and was not Judy thus proving herself worthy of their name and fame?

CHAPTER XXVII

THE SUMMER ENDS

In the softened light of the candles, the big mirrors reflected that night four misty groups of happy people.

A blur of pink down at one end, was Anne in rosy organdie, playing games with Tommy and Amelia and Nannie; a little fire flickered in the open grate, for the evening was cool, and one side of it sat the little grandmother and her old friend, the Judge, and on the other Dr. Grennell and Captain Jameson, engaged in an animated discussion; while in the window-seat, Judy and Launcelot gazed out upon the old garden.

"I shall miss it awfully," said Judy, with a little sigh.

Launcelot turned on her a startled glance.

"Why?" he asked, "where are you going?"

"Away to school," said Judy, "didn't Anne tell you?"

"Oh, I say - oh, I say, you're not, really?" Launcelot's voice had a queer break in it, that made Judy say quickly:

"We are coming back for Christmas."

"Well, this is my finish," said Launcelot, moved to slang, by the intensity of his feelings. "I thought it was bad enough to be cut out of going to college, but if you and Anne go away, I will give up."

"No, you won't," said Judy, quickly.

"Why not?"

"Because I should be so disappointed in you, Launcelot."

For a moment they looked at each other in silence. The light wind came in through the open window and stirred the laces of Judy's dress, and blew a wisp of dark hair across her earnest eyes, which shone with a depth of feeling that Launcelot had never seen there before, and as he looked, the boy was suddenly possessed with the spirit that animated the knights of old who yearned to prove themselves worthy of their ladies.

"Would you be disappointed, Judy?" he asked, very low.

"Yes," she leaned forward, speaking eagerly. "You - you don't know what this summer has meant to me, Launcelot. I came here so miserable, so unhappy, and I found you and Anne - and because you were both so brave when you have so many things to make life hard, I think it made me a little braver, and I could bear things better, because of you, and Anne, Launcelot.

"And so - I want always to think of you as brave," she went on, "I want to feel though there are cowards in the world, that you aren't one; though there are boys who fail and boys who are not what they ought to be, that you are really brave and true and good, Launcelot - always brave and true and good -"

For a moment he could not speak, and then he said in a moved voice:

"Do you really think that, Judy?"

"Really, Launcelot."

"It helps me to know it - it will help me all my life," he said, simply, and for a moment his hand touched hers, as if a promise were given and taken.

All his life he carried the picture of her as she sat there with the silver light of the moon making a halo for her head - and though after that she was many times her old tempestuous self, yet the vision of little St. Judith, as he named her then, stayed with him, and led him to the heights.

Judy went out to dinner on Dr. Grennell's arm. She looked very grown up with her long white dress, with her hair twisted high, with pearl sidecombs that had belonged to her grandmother, and with a bunch of violets - Launcelot's birthday gift to her, in her belt.

"How old are you, little lady?" asked the doctor, as they took their seats at the table.

"As old as I look," flashing a demure glance.

"Then you are ten," he decided, "in spite of your hair on top of your head. Your eyes give you away. They are child-eyes."

"I hope she will always keep child-eyes," said the Judge, who at the head of the table was serving the soup from an old-fashioned silver tureen, with Perkins at his elbow to pass the plates. "I don't want her to grow up."

"I shall always be your little girl, grandfather," and Judy nodded happily to him from the foot of the table, where she was taking Aunt Patterson's place, "even when I am forty."

"Aw, forty," said Tommy Tolliver, unexpectedly, "that's awful old. You'll be an old maid, Judy."

"That's what I intend to be," said that independent young lady. "I am going to be an artist."

"Oh, Judy," said little Anne, "you know you won't. You will marry Prince Charming and live happy ever after, as the fairy books say, and it will be lovely."

But Judy shrugged her shoulders, as they all laughed.

"We will see," she said, "and anyhow I am too young to think about such things," and at that the little grandmother nodded approval.

Tommy, having made his one contribution to the general conversation, ate steadily through the menu, accompanied by Amelia, whose sigh when the last course of ice-cream was served in little melons with candied cherries on top was expressive of great bliss.

But the crowning surprise of the dinner was the birthday cake.

Perkins brought it in on a great silver platter, and placed it in front of Judy with a flourish.

"Oh, oh, isn't it lovely," cried all the little girls.

"That's great," from Launcelot and Tommy.

"Perkins' *chef d'oeuvre*," was the Captain's comment, and the Judge and the doctor and Mrs. Batcheller added their praises.

It really was a beautiful cake. The icing foamed up all over it like waves, and on the very top of the sugary billows was placed a little candy sailboat, as nearly like the lost "Princess" as Perkins could procure.

"Oh, how perfectly beautiful," said Judy. "How did you think of it, Perkins?" and she smiled at him in a way that set his old heart a-beating.

"You're to cut it, Miss," he said, handing her a great silver-handled knife. "There's a ring in it, and a thimble and a piece

Temple Bailey

of money."

"Oh, I hope I'll get the ring," said little Anne, then blushed as Perkins said: "That means you'll get married, Miss."

"And the one who gets the thimble will work for a living, and the one who gets the money will be rich, isn't that it?" asked Judy, as she stuck the knife in. "Oh, it seems a shame to cut it, Perkins. It is so pretty."

Launcelot found the thimble in his slice, the money - a tiny gold dollar - was in Nannie's, while to Judy came the turquoise ring.

"You see you can't escape," said Launcelot, softly, as she turned the blue hoop on her finger. "Fate doesn't intend you for an artist."

"Well, I intend to be, whether fate does or not," she insisted. "I guess I can do as I please."

"Anne, you can have the thimble," said Launcelot, rolling it across the table-cloth to her. It was a beautiful little gold affair, and she loved to sew.

"I shouldn't mind being an old maid and working for a living," she said, surveying it contentedly, "if I could have Becky and Belinda to live with me."

"I'm glad I am going to be rich," said Nannie. "I shall travel and have a new dress every week."

"Huh," boasted Tommy, "I am going to get rich, if I didn't find the money in the cake."

"Sailors don't get rich," said the Captain. "It's a poor profession."

"Aw, a sailor," stammered Tommy, getting very red, "I'm not

going to be a sailor. I'm going to learn typewriting, and go to the city in an office."

And thus ended the Cause of Thomas, the Downtrodden!

But Amelia's plans proved the most interesting.

"I'm going to write," she announced, placidly. "I wrote a poem for Judy's birthday."

"Read it," they demanded, and Amelia, feeling very important, delivered the following:

"Oh, candy, oh, sugar, oh, cake, and oh, pie,
Are not half so sweet as dear J-U-D-Y."

It brought down the house, and Amelia was overcome by the honors heaped upon her.

"It isn't very good poetry," she confessed modestly, "but it means a lot."

And then the Captain made a little speech, in which he thanked Judy's friends for the happy summer she had spent among them. And then Launcelot made a speech and thanked Judy for the good times she had given them. And while Launcelot's speech wasn't as polished as the Captain's, it was so earnestly spoken that Judy was proud of her boy friend.

And after that they filed out to the old garden, the Judge and Mrs. Batcheller, and the Captain and Judy, Launcelot with his fair little friend Anne, and behind them the smaller fry, and Perkins - the wonderful Perkins at the end, with the coffee.

And there we will leave them, there in the old garden, where Judy had found hope and happiness, and where the little fountain sang ceaselessly to the nodding roses, of life and love, and of the things that had been and of the things that were to be.

Choose from Thousands of 1stWorldLibrary Classics By

A. M. Barnard
Ada Leverson
Adolphus William Ward
Aesop
Agatha Christie
Alexander Aaronsohn
Alexander Kielland
Alexandre Dumas
Alfred Gatty
Alfred Ollivant
Alice Duer Miller
Alice Turner Curtis
Alice Dunbar
Allen Chapman
Ambrose Bierce
Amelia E. Barr
Amory H. Bradford
Andrew Lang
Andrew McFarland Davis
Andy Adams
Anna Alice Chapin
Anna Sewell
Annie Besant
Annie Hamilton Donnell
Annie Payson Call
Annie Roe Carr
Annonaymous
Anton Chekhov
Arnold Bennett
Arthur Conan Doyle
Arthur M. Winfield
Arthur Ransome
Arthur Schnitzler
Atticus
B.H. Baden-Powell
B. M. Bower
B. C. Chatterjee
Baroness Emmuska Orczy
Baroness Orczy
Basil King
Bayard Taylor
Ben Macomber
Bertha Muzzy Bower
Bjornstjerne Bjornson
Booth Tarkington
Boyd Cable
Bram Stoker
C. Collodi
C. E. Orr

C. M. Ingleby
Carolyn Wells
Catherine Parr Traill
Charles A. Eastman
Charles Amory Beach
Charles Dickens
Charles Dudley Warner
Charles Farrar Browne
Charles Ives
Charles Kingsley
Charles Klein
Charles Hanson Towne
Charles Lathrop Pack
Charles Romyn Dake
Charles Whibley
Charles Willing Beale
Charlotte M. Braeme
Charlotte M. Yonge
Charlotte Perkins Stetson
Clair W. Hayes
Clarence Day Jr.
Clarence E. Mulford
Clemence Housman
Confucius
Coningsby Dawson
Cornelis DeWitt Wilcox
Cyril Burleigh
D. H. Lawrence
Daniel Defoe
David Garnett
Dinah Craik
Don Carlos Janes
Donald Keyhoe
Dorothy Kilner
Dougan Clark
Douglas Fairbanks
E. Nesbit
E.P.Roe
E. Phillips Oppenheim
Earl Barnes
Edgar Rice Burroughs
Edith Van Dyne
Edith Wharton
Edward Everett Hale
Edward J. O'Biren
Edward S. Ellis
Edwin L. Arnold
Eleanor Atkins
Eliot Gregory

Elizabeth Gaskell
Elizabeth McCracken
Elizabeth Von Arnim
Ellem Key
Emerson Hough
Emilie F. Carlen
Emily Dickinson
Enid Bagnold
Enilor Macartney Lane
Erasmus W. Jones
Ernie Howard Pie
Ethel May Dell
Ethel Turner
Ethel Watts Mumford
Eugenie Foa
Eugene Wood
Eustace Hale Ball
Evelyn Everett-green
Everard Cotes
F. H. Cheley
F. J. Cross
F. Marion Crawford
Federick Austin Ogg
Ferdinand Ossendowski
Francis Bacon
Francis Darwin
Frances Hodgson Burnett
Frances Parkinson Keyes
Frank Gee Patchin
Frank Harris
Frank Jewett Mather
Frank L. Packard
Frank V. Webster
Frederic Stewart Isham
Frederick Trevor Hill
Frederick Winslow Taylor
Friedrich Kerst
Friedrich Nietzsche
Fyodor Dostoyevsky
G.A. Henty
G.K. Chesterton
Gabrielle E. Jackson
Garrett P. Serviss
Gaston Leroux
George A. Warren
George Ade
Geroge Bernard Shaw
George Durston
George Ebers

George Eliot
George Gissing
George MacDonald
George Meredith
George Orwell
George Sylvester Viereck
George Tucker
George W. Cable
George Wharton James
Gertrude Atherton
Gordon Casserly
Grace E. King
Grace Gallatin
Grace Greenwood
Grant Allen
Guillermo A. Sherwell
Gulielma Zollinger
Gustav Flaubert
H. A. Cody
H. B. Irving
H.C. Bailey
H. G. Wells
H. H. Munro
H. Irving Hancock
H. Rider Haggard
H. W. C. Davis
Haldeman Julius
Hall Caine
Hamilton Wright Mabie
Hans Christian Andersen
Harold Avery
Harold McGrath
Harriet Beecher Stowe
Harry Castlemon
Harry Coghill
Harry Houidini
Hayden Carruth
Helent Hunt Jackson
Helen Nicolay
Hendrik Conscience
Hendy David Thoreau
Henri Barbusse
Henrik Ibsen
Henry Adams
Henry Ford
Henry Frost
Henry James
Henry Jones Ford
Henry Seton Merriman
Henry W Longfellow
Herbert A. Giles

Herbert Carter
Herbert N. Casson
Herman Hesse
Hildegard G. Frey
Homer
Honore De Balzac
Horace B. Day
Horace Walpole
Horatio Alger Jr.
Howard Pyle
Howard R. Garis
Hugh Lofting
Hugh Walpole
Humphry Ward
Ian Maclaren
Inez Haynes Gillmore
Irving Bacheller
Isabel Hornibrook
Israel Abrahams
Ivan Turgenev
J.G.Austin
J. Henri Fabre
J. M. Barrie
J. Macdonald Oxley
J. S. Fletcher
J. S. Knowles
J. Storer Clouston
Jack London
Jacob Abbott
James Allen
James Andrews
James Baldwin
James Branch Cabell
James DeMille
James Joyce
James Lane Allen
James Lane Allen
James Oliver Curwood
James Oppenheim
James Otis
James R. Driscoll
Jane Austen
Jane L. Stewart
Janet Aldridge
Jens Peter Jacobsen
Jerome K. Jerome
John Burroughs
John Cournos
John F. Kennedy
John Gay
John Glasworthy

John Habberton
John Joy Bell
John Kendrick Bangs
John Milton
John Philip Sousa
Jonas Lauritz Idemil Lie
Jonathan Swift
Joseph A. Altsheler
Joseph Carey
Joseph Conrad
Joseph E. Badger Jr
Joseph Hergesheimer
Joseph Jacobs
Jules Vernes
Julian Hawthrone
Julie A Lippmann
Justin Huntly McCarthy
Kakuzo Okakura
Kenneth Grahame
Kenneth McGaffey
Kate Langley Bosher
Kate Langley Bosher
Katherine Cecil Thurston
Katherine Stokes
L. A. Abbot
L. T. Meade
L. Frank Baum
Latta Griswold
Laura Dent Crane
Laura Lee Hope
Laurence Housman
Lawrence Beasley
Leo Tolstoy
Leonid Andreyev
Lewis Carroll
Lewis Sperry Chafer
Lilian Bell
Lloyd Osbourne
Louis Hughes
Louis Tracy
Louisa May Alcott
Lucy Fitch Perkins
Lucy Maud Montgomery
Luther Benson
Lydia Miller Middleton
Lyndon Orr
M. Corvus
M. H. Adams
Margaret E. Sangster
Margret Howth
Margaret Vandercook

Margret Penrose
Maria Edgeworth
Maria Thompson Daviess
Mariano Azuela
Marion Polk Angellotti
Mark Overton
Mark Twain
Mary Austin
Mary Catherine Crowley
Mary Cole
Mary Hastings Bradley
Mary Roberts Rinehart
Mary Rowlandson
M. Wollstonecraft Shelley
Maud Lindsay
Max Beerbohm
Myra Kelly
Nathaniel Hawthrone
Nicolo Machiavelli
O. F. Walton
Oscar Wilde
Owen Johnson
P.G. Wodehouse
Paul and Mabel Thorne
Paul G. Tomlinson
Paul Severing
Percy Brebner
Peter B. Kyne
Plato
R. Derby Holmes
R. L. Stevenson
R. S. Ball
Rabindranath Tagore
Rahul Alvares
Ralph Bonehill
Ralph Henry Barbour
Ralph Victor
Ralph Waldo Emmerson
Rene Descartes
Rex Beach

Rex E. Beach
Richard Harding Davis
Richard Jefferies
Richard Le Gallienne
Robert Barr
Robert Frost
Robert Gordon Anderson
Robert L. Drake
Robert Lansing
Robert Lynd
Robert Michael Ballantyne
Robert W. Chambers
Rosa Nouchette Carey
Rudyard Kipling
Samuel B. Allison
Samuel Hopkins Adams
Sarah Bernhardt
Sarah C. Hallowell
Selma Lagerlof
Sherwood Anderson
Sigmund Freud
Standish O'Grady
Stanley Weyman
Stella Benson
Stella M. Francis
Stephen Crane
Stewart Edward White
Stijn Streuvels
Swami Abhedananda
Swami Parmananda
T. S. Ackland
T. S. Arthur
The Princess Der Ling
Thomas A. Janvier
Thomas A Kempis
Thomas Anderton
Thomas Bailey Aldrich
Thomas Bulfinch
Thomas De Quincey
Thomas Dixon

Thomas H. Huxley
Thomas Hardy
Thomas More
Thornton W. Burgess
U. S. Grant
Valentine Williams
Various Authors
Vaughan Kester
Victor Appleton
Victoria Cross
Virginia Woolf
Wadsworth Camp
Walter Camp
Walter Scott
Washington Irving
Wilbur Lawton
Wilkie Collins
Willa Cather
Willard F. Baker
William Dean Howells
William le Queux
W. Makepeace Thackeray
William W. Walter
William Shakespeare
Winston Churchill
Yei Theodora Ozaki
Yogi Ramacharaka
Young E. Allison
Zane Grey

www.ingramcontent.com/pod-product-compliance
Lightning Source LLC
Chambersburg PA
CBHW020500100426
42813CB00030B/3061/J